exploding
humanity
the crisis of numbers

exploding humanity
the crisis of numbers

EDITED BY HENRY REGIER AND J. BRUCE FALLS

ANANSI   **TORONTO**   **1970**

First Printing 1969
Second Printing 1970

Printed in Canada

House of Anansi Press Limited
471 Jarvis Street
Toronto 284, Canada

ISBN: 0 88784 606 8 (paper); 0 88784 706 4 (cloth)

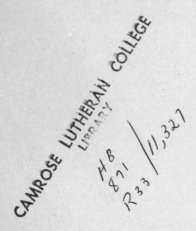

CONTENTS

PREFACE

This book is a record of a week-end conference – the Fourth International Teach-In – held in Varsity Arena, University of Toronto, on October 25 to 27, 1968. Over 3,000 people attended these sessions. The Teach-In followed a week of Pre-Teach-In events on campus – seminars in which various groups on campus discussed the topic in relation to their own insights, displays of contraceptives, films, lectures, wandering players, and a survey of undergraduate opinion on sex mores and population. All were products of a spontaneously organized, volunteer group of under-graduates, graduate students and professors at the University of Toronto. The purpose was educational: to focus critical, objective attention on many aspects of a serious national and international problem.

The major impetus came from a group of concerned ecologists in the Department of Zoology. They sought and obtained the sponsorship of the International Forum Foundation – a group of students, recent graduates, and professors – who had sponsored three previous Teach-Ins with much success. IFF, under the chairmanship of Dr. J.M. Robson, and with Mr. R. Gibson as treasurer, provided expert advice and lent their good name. The tasks of obtaining funds in excess of twenty thousand dollars, planning, organizing and effectuating the Teach-In were carried out by the volunteer 1968 Teach-In Committee.

The 1968 Committee very soon attracted collaborators from everywhere on campus. A total of more than 300 persons became actively involved for varying lengths of time. Special mention can be made of only a few of this large number. Dr. C.T. Bissell, President of the University of Toronto was honorary chairman; many other distinguished citizens lent their names to the honorary board. Dr. J.B. Falls was general chairman assisted by Dr. G.M. Clark. Drs. H.H. Harvey and W.G. Friend successfully managed the financial campaign. Dr. D.H. Pimlott and Mr. R.A. Stefanski organized ticket sales with the help of Messrs. D.R. Voigt, J.S. Loch and many others. Miss N.L. Harris and Dr. T.S. Parsons were co-chairmen of the publicity committee. Mr. R. Reoch designed posters and brochures and managed the campaign on campus. Mr. M.J. Kuttner provided liaison with the press; Mr. D.R.S. Lean was contact man with radio and television, with Miss M.E. Caldwell scheduling interviews. Miss D.W.M. Haden-Pawlowski

1

contacted outside organizations.

Drs. H.A. Regier and C.W. Schwenger led the programme committee which included, among others, Miss D.E. Dryer, Mr. M.G. Ignatieff, and Dr. A.E. Wingell. Messrs. W. E. Rees and M. Fitz-Earle organized the Pre-Teach-In events; many people co-operated in this undertaking, but special mention should be made of Dr. I. Malcolm whose play "And it came to pass that man began to multiply on the face of the earth" was performed by the Travelling Players of the Victoria College Drama Club. Miss A. Stiller and Dr. N. Mrosovsky organized a film programme for Saturday afternoon.

Mr. P.G. Wells assisted by Messrs. R. Davey, P. Craven, R.A.K. Richards, and Mrs. P. Lake co-ordinated the many activities of the arena committee. Guests were received and billeted, with charm and dispatch, by Miss M.C. Coburn. Misses S. Freeman and C. Chattin efficiently handled office affairs and Mr. W.V. Baker helped to mobilize personnel.

Financial assistance came from many sources, including the Ontario Government. The University of Toronto's contribution included use of many of its rooms and facilities gratis. The Department of Zoology was generous with both moral and material support.

The Teach-In proceedings were carried live on a large FM radio network extending across Canada, which the Canadian Broadcasting Corporation helped to make possible. Broadcasts originated with the Ryerson Institute of Technology's station CJRT managed by Mr. D. Stone and under the direction of Mr. R. McKee. Through the courtesy of Mr. D. Dale all sessions were videotaped and broadcast in subsequent weeks by station CHCH-TV in Hamilton, Ontario.

Mrs. Ann Falls and Dr. J.M. Robson assisted with the editing of these proceedings. Transcription of the audio tapes and most of the typing was done by Mrs. V. Howland of the Great Lakes Institute who was assisted by Mrs. C. Smith of the Department of Zoology.

J.B.F.
H.A.R.

Toronto
June 4, 1969

INTRODUCTION

Henry A. Regier and J. Bruce Falls

The number of people is increasing, and increasing at an increasing rate. Thus the quantity of humanity is accelerating. Can the quality of life and environment be maintained at acceptable levels if this trend continues?

In 1968 about 65 million was added to the number of people present in 1967, that is over three times the human population of Canada. There is no argument concerning the simple immediate cause of this phenomenal growth — death rates have been reduced greatly in a short period of time and birth rates have on the whole declined much less rapidly. A few decades ago most persons born did not live to reproduce, now most are able to do so.

The more basic causes and effects of the population increase are like a tangled knot. Though basically a biological phenomenon it interacts with virtually every other area of human existence and, according to some observers, renders every human problem more difficult to solve. In organizing the Teach-In programme, of which this book is the proceedings, we were struck by the diversity of views we encountered. Some felt that if only enough food could be produced there would be no population problem and suggested suitable speakers holding such a viewpoint. Others saw it chiefly as a question of political and economic development. For some the moral and religious problems loomed large. More "radical" persons were preoccupied with political and ideological confrontation. Women's rights and the rights of minorities were stressed. The importance of medical experts to discuss contraceptive methods was urged. Our biological colleagues looked for a strong emphasis on emerging ecological ideas. The programme finally accepted was the product of such a diverse set of viewpoints. The title—Exploding Humanity—was selected because it, too, has a diverse set of possible connotations.

Topics were formulated and organized in the format as shown in the Table of Contents. Speakers were chosen for their outstanding competence in their own fields and for their abilities to communicate their ideas to a varied audience. Short biographical sketches are given for each—at the beginning of the relevent chapter—so that the reader may gain additional understanding of the views expressed.

The Chairmen of the four sessions were Father Gregory Baum, the Rev. Dr. Frank Fidler, Mr. George W. Cadbury, and the Honourable Donald C. Macdonald. Short biographical sketches of them may be found on page 7.

Each speaker submitted a paper before the Teach-In began. It was intended that these papers be published almost verbatim. However a number of speakers, notably Drs. Carstairs, Clark, and Borgstrom, deviated rather markedly from the prepared speech including additional highly interesting and relevant material. We resolved the resulting editorial problem in the following manner: for Dr. Carstairs' speech we collated paragraphs of the prepared and extempore versions; for Dr. Clark's contribution we appended most of the extempore speech to the end of the submitted paper; for Dr. Borgstrom's chapter we chose the extempore speech and collated with it a few paragraphs of the prepared version. For all other speakers the editing chores were minor.

Much of the discussion following each of the four sessions is included in the book. After the major addresses, any person in the audience had free access to a microphone on the floor to address the meeting. Editing of the discussion transcripts involved mostly deletion of repetitive passages and the occasional quite technical discussion on some more distantly related matter.

The discussions as reproduced here include, in a number of cases, edited transcripts of a radio panel broadcasting from a booth in Varsity Arena immediately after the conclusion of proceedings on the floor. Participants on the radio panel provided critical comment or additional insights on the subject discussed in that session.

To some persons *Teach-In* means *confrontation* and there were instances of sharp confrontation at the 1968 Teach-In. But the Teach-Ins sponsored by the International Forum Foundation are chiefly *educational* in nature. The really important confrontation hoped for is one between each person and the problem. Each of us, after all, is a basic component in the population explosion. Each of us has to face up to it. This book does not provide a neat resolution of conflicting viewpoints. It does hopefully provide relevant material necessary for a reasoned decision as to what if anything should be done. But the decision will depend ultimately on the nature of the reader's system of values.

Many have asked if the 1968 Teach-In was a success. We have no good measure of its impact. The idea for this Teach-In arose from our concern that accelerating population growth would enormously increase human misery and bring about environmental deterioration—a threatening doom in the face of which we felt helpless as individuals. We decided to inform ourselves and others about this problem with the hope that information would lead to consensus and to concerted action. The format of a Teach-In seemed to provide a suitably dramatic medium. Yet, we had no illusions that it would have dramatic practical effects.

Recently, a series of articles in a Canadian newspaper celebrated the growth of our own cities—50,000 a year added to Toronto—an exciting city! Few Canadians as yet identify current domestic problems of our cities (housing shortages, traffic congestion, air pollution, rising crime rates) or of the countryside (polluted lakes, disappearing farmlands, fewer natural areas, less space for recreation) with population problems.

On the other side, the criminal code has been amended so that it is no longer a crime to disseminate information about contraceptives; planned parenthood may soon be an option for all Canadians and not just for the affluent. Our external aid programme is under review—perhaps in future we shall take population problems into account in seeking to help others.

Closer to home two new courses on aspects of human ecology have been added to the University of Toronto curriculum; a student organization called "Pollution Probe" is concerning itself with the quality of our environment; the thinking and careers of some of those involved in the Teach-In have been reoriented; groups in other cities and lands have contacted us about sponsoring Teach-Ins in their own areas on population and pollution. Articles on population have appeared in several Canadian conservation periodicals and articles on conservation have appeared in a planned parenthood publication. The Teach-In may have helped to precipitate these and other events.

Population problems will be with us for a long time to come. At the time of writing, an economist of the OECD has stated that they may be more difficult to deal with than had formerly been supposed. In a letter written to us before the Teach-In, Julian Huxley emphasized the need for greater awareness of the impending danger to civilization and human fulfilment posed by the population explosion. He concluded "I feel sure that your Teach-In will make an important contribution to this awareness." If it has helped to begin a serious consideration of these questions in Canada, we shall be well satisfied that it was worth the effort.

About the Chairmen of the Sessions

Father Gregory Baum, a member of the Augustinian Order, originally studied mathematics and physics at McMaster University before embarking on a theological career. Now at St. Michael's College, he is a world renowned theologian who has held a number of high posts in the Church, particularly with the Secretariat for Promoting Christian Unity and as a consultant at the Second Vatican Council.

The Rev. Dr. Frank P. Fidler is a United Church of Canada minister, at present Associate Secretary of the Board of Education of the United Church. He studied theology at Emmanuel College after taking a degree in Engineering at the University of Manitoba. He is Past-President of the National Council of Churches in Canada and President of the Family Planning Federation of Canada.

Mr. George W. Cadbury studied at Cambridge. He came to Canada in 1945 and spent some years working with the Government of Saskatchewan. He was later Director of Organization in the Technical Assistance Administration of the United Nations. For some years Mr. and Mrs. Cadbury were international representatives of the International Planned Parenthood Federation, travelling the world over; Mr. Cadbury is now Chairman of the Executive Committee of that organization. He is an officer of the New Democratic Party of Canada.

The Honourable Donald S. Macdonald is President of the Privy Council of the Government of Canada. He has represented the riding of Rosedale, Toronto in the House of Commons since 1962. He studied at the University of Toronto, Harvard, Cambridge, and Osgoode Hall.

About the Editors

J. Bruce Falls is Professor of Zoology at the University of Toronto. He studied at the University of Toronto and at Oxford University. His research interest is in behavioural ecology. Dr. Falls has been active in a number of conservation organizations. He is co-chairman of the International Biological Programme's conservation panel for Ontario, past-president of the Federation of Ontario Naturalists, a member of the Conservation Council of Ontario, and a member of the Advisory Committee on Nature Reserves to the Ontario Minister of Lands and Forests. He married E. Ann Holmes and they have three children. Dr. Falls was general chairman of the 1968 Teach-In.

Henry A. Regier is Associate Professor of Zoology at the University of Toronto. His research interests are in the ecology of aquatic communities. He studied at Queen's University and Cornell University. Dr.

Regier investigated Lake Erie problems for a number of years as a scientist with the Ontario Department of Lands and Forests. He has been a consultant with the Great Lakes Fishery Commission, is now on the executive committee of Planned Parenthood of Toronto, and is an advisor to Pollution Probe. He married H. Lynn Dyck and they have three children. Dr. Regier was programme chairman of the 1968 Teach-In.

FIRST SESSION
THE RACE AGAINST EXTINCTION

OUR MAN-MADE ENVIRONMENTAL CRISIS

Lamont C. Cole

Lamont C. Cole was born in Chicago in 1916. He studied physics at the University of Chicago, then biology at the University of Utah, and finally ecology at the University of Chicago where he was awarded the Ph.D. in 1944.

After serving as an officer of the U.S. Public Health Service for two years, Dr. Cole joined the faculty of Indiana University and, a year later, went to Cornell University where he is Professor of Ecology.

Dr. Cole has published many papers on ecological topics, often emphasizing the need for rigorous application of the scientific method in ecological studies.

Professor Cole has served in numerous capacities on committees and agencies with special concerns in human population problems and environmental biology. These include the U.S. National Institutes of Health, National Science Foundation, Ecological Society of America, American Institute of Biological Sciences, National Academy of Sciences, etc. He is an articulate leader and spokesman for the ecological viewpoint on U.S. national policies.

Ecologists represent a small group of persons who try to anticipate the effects of environmental changes before we make these changes. Unfortunately, these changes are often subtle and slow, and most of mankind is impatient to get on with changing the world whether by physical and chemical means or by dispersing exotic plants and animals. Man has created most of his problems.

As a single example consider the Welland Canal, which permitted the herring-like alewife and the parasitic sea lamprey to enter the upper Great Lakes. The alewife became a valuable forage fish for lake trout, which were the basis for commercial fisheries yielding millions of dollars annually. But the lamprey helped destroy the commercial fishery by killing off the lake trout and also the whitefish. With their predators gone, the alewives multiplied without restraint with the result that for the past two summers newspapers have carried pictures of dead alewives polluting Chicago and Milwaukee beaches. Since the original Welland Canal was opened in 1824 and the present canal dates from 1932, in this case it took at least thirty years and perhaps more than a century for the disastrous consequences of an engineering project to become evident.

Man has been changing his environment almost from the beginning. Neolithic man probably used fire as a tool first to drive game and later to clear forests for grazing. By an incredible stroke of luck the grasslands which were created by fire and maintained by fire and grazing developed soils that eventually made them among the world's most valuable agricultural lands. In large part our North American prairies fall in this category, as do large grassland and savannah areas of Africa.

Of course smoke polluted the atmosphere, but man had already seen this happen from natural fires. The burning of vegetation on slopes led to erosion that polluted streams and sometimes blocked them, producing swamps and marshes.

Later, man began his serious agricultural efforts on the flood plains of rivers where the land was well watered and easy to work with simple tools. As populations grew he felt the need for more land and year-round cultivation. He built dams and canals for irrigation and established great civilizations. But he often failed to provide for adequate drainage, with the result that water moved upward through the soil, evaporated there and deposited dissolved salts on the surface, thus destroying fertility. Burning, cultivation, and the grazing of slopes caused erosion so that the irrigation works filled with silt and the civilizations collapsed. Modern Iraq could not feed the once great Babylonian Empire, nor could modern Iran, without its income from oil, support the Persian Empire of Darius I.

Man's earliest industrial efforts created unrecognized pollution problems; similar practices still are carried on, yet many people refuse to acknowledge the problems. The Romans mined lead in Britain and smelted it there, and it is said that the sites of those old smelting operations are still recognizable from the impoverished vegetation growing on the poisoned soil. In Rome the lead went into paints and water pipes and to line the vessels in which wine was stored. Recent studies of Roman bones have shown concentrations of lead that indicate that many members of the upper classes must have suffered from lead poisoning—it has been suggested that this may have contributed to the decline of the Empire. But we refuse to learn. Modern industry and the burning of ethyl gasoline are putting tremendous quantities of lead into our environment. A recent study of old elm trees showed a rapidly increasing concentration of lead in the wood produced since about 1937, and a study of snow near the North Pole has shown a 300 percent increase in lead content since about 1940.

When man started contaminating the world his impact went unnoticed, but by the twelfth century we find contemporary accounts of severe air and water pollution, for example the "poisonous vapors" of

Rome and the "lethal waters" of the river Rhine (a name incidentally supposedly derived from the German word for "clear"). But man created a new dimension of environmental deterioration when he began serious exploitation of the fossil fuels, peat, coal, natural gas, and, more recently, petroleum.

It is recorded that in the year 1306 a citizen of London was tried and executed for burning coal in the city. But three centuries later this was the way of life and London had a smog problem. The profession of chimney sweeping was born and along with it one of the earliest and most striking examples of severe industrial pathology; cancer of the scrotum induced by exposure to soot. It is interesting to note that Los Angeles has recently banned the burning of coal in the city, so man has in a sense come full circle on this one problem.

We are now so dependent on fossil fuels that surveys have found farmers expending more calories running their machinery than are removed from their land in crops. Industrial plants, transportation, especially by automobile, and the heating requirements of an expanding world population have brought the combustion of fossil fuels to the point where we are actually causing measurable changes in the composition of the earth's atmosphere. And, as we shall see, we are risking much more serious changes in the atmosphere than anything noted so far.

And never before has man been able to spread particular pollutants over the entire surface of the earth. DDT is a case in point; it has been found in the fat of Antarctic seals and penguins, in the fatty tissues of fish all over the world, and in the ice of Alaskan glaciers. We have simply been incredibly lucky that DDT has not turned out to be a more noxious pollutant than it is because, if it had happened to possess certain properties that no one would have known about until it was too late, it could have brought an end to life on earth.

If you find it comforting that DDT is not as bad as it might have been, reflect on the fact that the U.S. Food and Drug Administration estimates that we are now exposing ourselves to over a half-million different chemicals all of which must eventually be imposed on the earth's environment, and the number is estimated to be increasing by from 400 to 500 per year.

Consider the completely novel types of materials we have asked the environment to assimilate just since World War II: synthetic pesticides, plastics, anti-biotics, radioisotopes, detergents. The detergents provide an instructive case. A few years ago people could see this pollution and they were agonizing because suds were coming out of their faucets. The answer was to turn to the so-called "biodegradable" detergents, and the public relaxed, considering the problem solved. They don't realize that

11

the new detergents are more toxic than the old visible ones to many forms of aquatic life, or that these detergents are phosphorus compounds, and that phosphorus is one of our most significant water pollutants.

We are at most a few generations away from running out of the fossil fuels on which our economy, including agriculture, now depends. Current thinking holds that our next source of energy will be nuclear fuel, but this raises some very disturbing thoughts. Before the controlled release of atomic energy the total amount of radioactive material under human control consisted of about 10 grams of radium, or 10 curies of radioactivity. Probably a billion times this amount of radioactivity has already been disseminated into the environment, and we are not really yet into the atomic age. A plant of modest size (by present dreams) is being constructed on the shores of Lake Ontario near Oswego, New York, that will, by the Company's own estimate, release to the atmosphere 130 curies per day. Knowing that exposure to radioactivity shortens life, causes malignancies, and can produce genetic effects that can damage future generations, have we cause for complacency?

Few people apparently realize that our atmosphere is a biological product that has probably remained essentially unchanged in composition for at least 300 million years, right up until the present century. Neglecting contaminants, the atmosphere at sea level consists of about 78 percent nitrogen by volume, 21 percent oxygen, and 0.03 percent carbon dioxide plus minor amounts of other gases I shall not consider here.

Nitrogen is actually a scarce element on earth. Eighteen elements account for 99.9 percent of the mass of all known terrestrial matter, and nitrogen is not among the 18. What is so much of it doing in the atmosphere? Oxygen is the most abundant of all the chemical elements but it is a highly reactive chemical which, aside from the atmosphere, almost never exists in the uncombined form. What is so much free oxygen doing in the atmosphere? The answers to both questions are biological.

Certain bacteria and algae take nitrogen from the atmosphere and convert it into ammonia which is quite a toxic substance. If the story stopped at this stage we should all be fatally poisoned when we breathe. Two additional kinds of microorganisms in soil and water are responsible for converting the ammonia to nitrate, and green plants absorb the nitrate and use its nitrogen in building plant proteins. Animals, including ourselves, and virtually the entire world of microorganisms, obtain the raw materials for building their own proteins directly or indirectly from the proteins of plants. When plants and animals die, the decomposer organisms, again primarily microorganisms, break down the proteins, mostly to ammonia, and this little cycle—ammonia to nitrate, nitrate to protein, protein to ammonia—can repeat. If the story stopped at this stage

12

the atmosphere would long ago have run out of nitrogen. Fortunately, there are still additional types of microorganisms that can convert nitrate to molecular nitrogen and so maintain the composition of the atmosphere.

So we can see that quite a variety of microorganisms involved in the nitrogen cycle are essential for the continuation of life. But what thought does industrialized man give to the welfare of these forms? With reckless abandon he dumps his half-million chemicals into soil, water, and air, not knowing whether or not one of these chemicals or some combination of them might be a deadly poison for one of the steps in the nitrogen cycle and so cause the extinction of life on earth. In fact I have heard serious suggestions from chemically sophisticated but ecologically ignorant persons for deliberately blocking two of the steps in the nitrogen cycle. How long can our luck continue?

There is oxygen in our atmosphere only because green plants keep putting it there. The plants take in carbon dioxide and give off oxygen, and animals and microorganisms take in oxygen and give off carbon dioxide. So do our factories, our furnaces, and our automobiles. Seventy percent of the free oxygen produced each year comes from planktonic diatoms in the oceans. But what thought does man give to the diatoms when he disposes of his wastes? When he wants a new highway, factory, housing project, or strip mine he is not even solicitous of the green plants growing on land. The fate of Lake Erie and many lesser bodies of water has shown us that man is indeed capable of blocking the oxygen cycle by sheer carelessness.

If this leaves you complacent, let me mention just a few more of the details. The deciduous forests of the eastern United States appear to produce about 1,000 times as much oxygen per unit area as the average cover of the earth's surface. Yet forests seem to be the things that modern man is willing to dispense with first. Tropical rain forests, unlike our deciduous forests, carry on photosynthesis of oxygen throughout the year and so are probably considerably more productive. But several times each year I read of schemes for industrializing or otherwise "developing" the tropical regions of Latin America, Africa, and Asia. I recently read a statement by the President of Brazil to the effect that we must get on with developing the Amazon basin.

Tropical soils are typically low in mineral nutrients and such minerals as are present leach from the soil quickly if the vegetation is unable to trap them and recycle them. Hence, when a tropical forest is destroyed, the change may be irreversible. I don't think any educated and responsible person would advocate applying defoliants and herbicides to a tropical forest without first making a careful survey of the nutrient status of the soil and vegetation. But ecological understanding is not a

13

prerequisite for policy making!

In the United States today the military is taking 100 percent of the production of the so-called weed killer 2,4,5T; they are taking about one-third of the production of 2,4D and they are taking the entire production of a newer and much deadlier weed killer known as Picloram. Picloram is awful stuff. When you spray it on vegetation, typically nothing grows for two years. We have a case in Vermont where mules fed on vegetation that had been sprayed by Picloram; a year later when manure from these mules was used as fertilizer, it killed all the plants it was put on. Now our government is negotiating to build new plants to step up the production of this stuff. What are they going to do with it? They are going to put it in tankers and ship it to Vietnam to defoliate the rain forest so that they can see the Viet Cong easier and also, they hope, kill rice.

Similarly, in the seas, estuaries tend to be much more productive than either the land adjacent to them or most of the open ocean. In Georgia we actually have figures that the estuaries and salt marshes are two or three times as productive of life as the best agricultural land in the State. They not only produce oxygen but also serve as the nursery grounds for the immature stages of species we harvest for seafood. Yet estuaries are where coastal man is likely to dump his refuse, and they are the places where commercial developers are constantly undertaking land fill and dredging operations. They are also among the places where it is proposed to locate huge electrical generating plants which would raise the temperature of the water and, in some cases, pollute it with radioisotopes. But who is thinking of the welfare of the green plants, or the organisms involved in the nitrogen cycle, or of other types of organisms essential for man's survival?

As a corollary of our rapid use of oxygen and our threats to the species that produce it, we are adding carbon dioxide to the atmosphere more rapidly than the oceans can assimilate it. This has serious implications for changing the climate of the earth, but since the details are still so uncertain and controversial I shall not go into them here. But one point I do wish to put in the form of a question: Would any rational creature go on changing his environment like this without understanding the possible effects, and at the same time argue that it is necessary to keep the destructive process expanding each year? What is now popularly known as "progress" begins to look very much like the path to extinction.

I have attempted some quantitative calculations on the oxygen cycle in order to see where we stand. For the forty-eight coterminous States of the U.S., I took the figures for the production and imports of fossil fuels for the year 1966, corrected the figures for exports and for non-combustible residues, and calculated the amount of oxygen consumed in

14

their combustion. Then I made what I believe is the best possible estimate of the amount of oxygen produced in the forty-eight States that year through green plant photosynthesis. The estimate of oxygen produced turned out to be not quite 60 percent of the oxygen consumed. I have no doubt that one would reach similar conclusions for other heavily industrialized nations.

The implication is clear; we are absolutely dependent upon atmospheric circulation patterns to bring in oxygen produced outside our borders, probably mostly in the Pacific Ocean. If we should inadvertently kill enough of the diatoms in the Pacific we would start running out of oxygen to breathe. Think again about those tankers carrying Picloram to Vietnam. I don't know what Picloram does to marine diatoms, probably nobody has considered it worth looking into, but from what it does to vegetation on land I take a very pessimistic view of it. If a few of those tankers should be sunk in the Pacific we might have an instant crisis. If we should seriously attempt to industrialize all of the nations of the earth after our own pattern, I think we would all perish for lack of oxygen before the transition was nearly complete.

I've been discussing the atmosphere without unnatural contaminants. I'm sure you all know the true situation—that over 3000 foreign chemicals have been chemically identified in our atmosphere—that, in our cities, particulate matter, soot, fly ash and, perhaps more importantly particles of rubber and asbestos, pose a serious public health problem—that carbon monoxide, sulphur dioxide, and the various nitrogen oxides pose more problems. Our intense agricultural efforts are themselves causing some ironic difficulties. A few years ago there was an amusing debate running in an Iowa paper. It involved a law case in which the defendant was claiming that 2,4D should be considered a normal constituent of the Iowa atmosphere during summer. Similarly phosphorus is in such short supply and so badly needed for fertilizer that we permit severe damage to the environment by plants that process phosphate rock into phosphate fertilizer. In Florida and in several of the western states the fluorine which is produced as a by-product of this process has killed vegetation for long distances around the plant and has killed stock animals eating the plants. In Florida there was a law suit asking the company to put higher stacks on the plant. This of course would not reduce the pollution but would spread it a little more widely. The company argued that this was not practicable because fluorine is so corrosive that the taller stacks would corrode too rapidly. So human lungs are being asked to take what mortar and concrete can't.

Underlying all of our other problems is the problem of unrestrained population growth. During the first million years or so of man's existence his population doubled perhaps once every fifty thousand years. Sometime during the summer of 1968, the human population of the earth passed the 3.5 billion mark, and if present trends could continue the population would double every thirty-five years.

There is no possibility that the earth can continue to support such growth. In fact I doubt that the earth can support on a sustained basis a population as large as the present one. In the last quarter century man's impact on the earth has grown to the point where there is a real possibility that he can destroy its ability to support life.

So, through the eyes of an ecologist, the world environment is in a desperate condition. In the United States, as I write we are approaching the end of an election campaign, and I am one ecologist waiting with despairing frustration to learn that the candidates appreciate the really important problems, and what they propose to do about them.

What measures will be taken to stop population growth in the United States and to help other nations solve their population problems? What blue ribbon panel will consider whether our population is already too large, and how the growth trend may be reversed? Can anyone doubt that our problems of pollution and urban unrest are related to overcrowding?

It is estimated that in the United States the production of trash is increasing by between four and five percent each year which by no accident is just about equal to the annual growth of the gross national product.

Who will reaffirm that we shall never again be the first to use nuclear weapons, tactical or otherwise? How can we get France and China to stop atmospheric testing — and how can we prevent the spread of nuclear capability to unstable governments that may come under the control of fanatics?

What steps will be taken to reverse the alarming deterioration of our environment?

Can't we outlaw chemical and biological warfare? In this area the big powerful nation has little advantage over a small impoverished neighbour. I'm confident that Cuba can't build a hydrogen bomb, but she can build an anthrax bomb. What political leader will commit himself to preventing such developments?

Finally, how are the oceans to be used wisely? Industrial giants are just discovering that there is wealth besides seafood to be obtained from the oceans and their bottoms. Will another colonial-type race be allowed to develop for these resources?

Who will bring together the biologists, physical scientists, sociologists, economists, and political scientists who, if we are to survive, simply must learn to communicate with each other and to recommend policy decisions on such matters? Where do our candidates stand? Where do any of the world leaders stand?

I will leave it to you to decide whether there are grounds for optimism.

EDITORS' NOTE. Since this address was delivered, there has been considerable controversy concerning the extent to which the world's oxygen supply is threatened by human activities. Readers wishing to pursue this subject may find the following references helpful:

Broeker, W.S. (1970). Man's oxygen reserves. *Science, 168*, 1537.

Cole, L.C. (1968). Can the world be saved? *Bioscience, 18*, 679.

Ryther, J.H. (1970). Is the world's oxygen supply threatened? *Nature, 227*, 374.

We understand that further articles on this subject, including one by Dr. Cole, will appear in the November-December, 1970 issue of the magazine *Environment*. For general background, readers might consult articles on oxygen and carbon in the September, 1970 issue of *Scientific American* which was devoted to "The Biosphere".

RELATIONSHIP OF ECONOMICS TO THE POLITICS OF POPULATION DYNAMICS AND POPULATION CONTROL

Errol Walton Barrow

Errol Walton Barrow was born in St. Andrew Parish, Barbados in 1920. His father is the Rev. Reginald Grant Barrow, a clergyman of the Anglican Church; his mother was Ruth O'Neale, sister of Dr. Charles Duncan O'Neale who was the founder of the Patriotic League and a member of the Barbados House of Assembly. Mr. Barrow married Caroline Plaskett of New Jersey in 1945; they have a son and a daughter.

Mr. Barrow was a member of the Royal Air Force in World War II. He was personal Navigation Officer to the Commander-in-Chief of the British Army of the Rhine.

He studied economics and political science at the University of London and was called to the bar at The Inns of Court in 1949.

From 1951 to 1955 Mr. Barrow was a member of the Barbados Labour Party and then became a co-founder of the Democratic Labour Party. He is Prime Minister of Barbados and holds several other portfolios including External Affairs and Finance.

Just before I left my island home yesterday morning I was horrified to read in the local newspaper that the University of Toronto was mounting the largest exhibition of the use of contraceptives ever known to mankind, that the students were being invited to answer a questionnaire relating their own experiences, and that the Prime Minister of the Barbados was one of the experts being invited to speak. Having made a careful check I have discovered that this "misleading" report came from one of the internationally well known news agencies.

In discussing the relationship of economics to the politics of population dynamics and population control, especially in the developing countries, I should like to make it clear that I am speaking in very general terms and presenting my own views and not necessarily those of the Government of Barbados.

The relationship of economics to population growth came under serious study in the first half of the nineteenth century, and inspired the economists of the day to make such gloomy forecasts of the fate of mankind that the study of economics was promptly labelled the "dismal science". This was the era that produced the "wages fund" theory. The iron law of wages naturally produced the Malthusian concepts that population tended to outrun food supply since one increased in geometric and the other in arithmetic progression, and that, unless moral and physical restraint were exercised, the only possible alternatives were pestilence, disease, famine and war, the end result of which would be the enforced limitation of population numbers by increased mortality.

The Reverend Dr. Malthus can claim, with some degree of justification, to be the father of population control concepts, particularly the concepts which have become more readily acceptable to the Church. From late marriage and self-restraint to rhythm has been a less startling development than from the prophylactic to the pill.

The Malthusian analysis was speedily accepted without further examination by the expatriate Marx, living in London but prognosticating from premises predominantly Prussian, and offering bloody revolution as a solution to the inevitable economic bondage implicit in the prevailing philosophy. Marx therefore completed the eighteenth century triangulation of population growth and control, economics, and politics, since he suggested that an overthrow of existing political institutions would automatically bring about a solution of the economic problem by equalising the distribution of a country's wealth.

The logic and scientific method of economics and demography have improved and changed beyond recognition since the days of Malthus and Marx. They are now backed up by a limitless fund of statistical material, more careful scientific research, and the availability of more knowledge about the influence of technological innovation.

The truth is that all the nations whose economies and political institutions came under critical analysis in the earlier half of the nineteenth century were developing nations. They were essentially pre-technological societies which had not fully understood or accepted in their entirety the consequences of the industrial revolution that had been evident as early as the middle of the eighteenth century.

The rates of technological change and of population growth from 1760 to 1860 were immeasurably less than the rates that have been produced in the first sixty years alone of the twentieth century. But what is most significant about the twentieth century is that the gap between the developed countries and the developing nations is an ever-widening one, accentuated further by marked differences in population growth rates and attitudes, both social and political, to population control.

In the developed countries the "demographic revolution" has been

20

achieved with rates of economic growth well in advance of rates of population growth: with increases in non-human resources more than adequate to cater for increases in human resources, and an age structure of population, with low dependency ratio, favourable to economic development. The population problem in these countries is really one of the unrestricted growth of huge urban conurbations—megalopolis. Similarly, population control is only an issue at the personal level—i.e., it is a matter of conscience—that arises in any case only in particular religious groups, especially Catholics. Voluntary limitation is practised widely, and *"desired"* size of family, from the individual's point of view, corresponds fairly closely with *"desirable"* size of family, from the point of view of the nation as a whole.

The population problem in less developed countries is of a different order of magnitude. There are two aspects of the problem, one static, the other dynamic.

(a) The *static* aspect of the problem concerns the absolute size of the population base, and its relation in the short-run to the supply of other resources, particularly land. A primary question, there, is the "density" of population. Most less developed countries are not characterized by high population densities: e.g., though many parts of Asia have high densities, many parts of Latin America and Asia are very sparsely peopled. But for a particular group of less developed countries – small island communities like those we have in the Caribbean and in Mauritius, for example—the problem of density is of great significance. Classical economists spoke of "optimum" population size, the assumption being that given fixed supplies of land, capital and technology, for every community there existed a "correct" or "optimum" size of population. Today we know that (in theory at least) this is false, since capital and technology can be increased to compensate for lack of land or natural resources. However, for less developed countries with great population densities, it is not so easy to increase the supply of capital or technology, *since a condition of underdevelopment is that capital is scarce and technology backward*. So that for these communities, the static question of density is as important as the dynamic question of rate of population growth: this vital point should not be lost sight of in talk of a "population explosion". In Barbados, for example, the absolute size of the population base is of very great importance; because of the high labour/land ratio, opportunities for increasing employment on the land are necessarily limited, and the development of secondary industries is a necessity; yet the small size of the population base (which is relatively large for the area of land which we have) inhibits industrial growth, because of the small extent of the market (only a quarter of a million persons).

21

(b) The *dynamic* aspect of the population problem concerns the annual rate of change of the population base. This raises the Malthusian spectre in the less developed countries. Annual rates of growth of the gross domestic product of three to five percent are accompanied by annual rates of growth of population of two to three percent (the result in most cases of high and stable birth rates and falling death rates). In some cases the increase in output of goods and services is barely keeping pace with the increase in the number of mouths to be fed, and even in those cases where the gross domestic product may be growing faster than the population, the margin is so slender that living standards would be rising by only a meagre one to one and one-half percent per annum, and this from a palpably low level.

Other well known aspects of rapid population growth which must be taken into account are:

(i) Increase in consumption at the expense of investment (i.e., less resources being devoted in the present to increasing consumption in the future), which further reduces rates of economic growth.

(ii) Changing age-structure of the population: an increase in "dependency ratio" or the percentage of under-15's in the population; a decrease in the percentage of those in the productive age groups (i.e., those in the labour force). The result is a distribution of investment inimical to rapid economic growth, away from productive projects and into welfare and social avenues (e.g., baby clinics, day nurseries, hospitals, and investment for school places rather than investment to change the quality of education).

(iii) The result of this changed age-structure will be a rapid build-up of the labour force in the near future, as the children now born, who survive, leave school. This accentuates an already grave unemployment problem, caused by the fact that the "traditional" sector (peasant agriculture, petty trades, domestic service) is losing labour faster than the "modern" sector (commercial agriculture, industry, tourism) can absorb it. In fact, if rates of population growth continue to press on rates of economic growth, the economy will be like a man on a treadmill, exerting pressure to move on, but in fact standing still.

We all agree, therefore, that even where the *absolute size* of population is no problem, rates of growth have to be curbed if standards of living are to be raised to acceptable levels.

In the considerable controversy that surrounds this issue of population control one can discern two main schools of thought. There are those who say that the first priority should be to raise the material standards of living, and that fertility will decline automatically as a result; and there are those who stress the urgency of reducing fertility as a precondition to increased economic growth. As in most of these cases, the truth would seem to lie somewhere in between. On the one hand, rising income levels and economic development generally are powerful inducements to reduced fertility because of the effects on the structure of the family which the concomitants of growth bring—viz., increased education, urbanization, strengthening of the "nuclear" as opposed to the "extended" family, and most important perhaps, *the increased involvement of women in the labour force*. All these factors tend towards smaller families. On the other hand, there is now a widespread belief that direct appeals to individuals to limit the size of families through the agency of family planning programmes can be effective. It is now known that the notion that poor people want large families for economic reasons is in many cases quite false, and that the citizens of underdeveloped countries desperately want to prevent unwanted births and to raise their living standards.

It must be admitted, however, that it is extremely difficult to measure the effectiveness of these programmes, and that often claims made on their behalf are exaggerated. It has been pointed out that most of these programmes are *partial* in approach (they do not for example, advocate *all* types of birth control, like sterilization) and they seek only to reduce the *actual* size of family to the *desired* size of family, even though the *desired* size of family (from the individual viewpoint) is still much larger in most less developed countries than the *desirable* size of family (from the national viewpoint). These programmes also tend to avoid giving advice to unmarried women and young girls for fear of being accused of encouraging promiscuity. Yet it is among these groups that the proliferation of live births occurs in developing countries.

Barbados is an interesting case study in the context of this controversy. Barbados had one of the first family planning programmes in the Western Hemisphere (1957). Between 1920 and 1963, our crude birth rate was in the vicinity of 33 per 1,000—high by the standards of developed countries, but fairly modest by standards of some less developed countries (where 40-50 per 1,000 is not uncommon). From 1964, however, our crude birth rate has fallen gradually to 22 per 1,000, now below the figure for even some developed countries.

Now the crude birth rate is not necessarily an accurate index of fertility trends, but research being carried out (by staff at the University of the West Indies) indicates that the fall in crude birth rate is the result of two factors:

(i) *Emigration.* This affected the age and sex structure of the population (since most of the migrants tend to be males aged 15-49).

(ii) *Voluntary limitation.* Here, the effect of the family planning programme in spreading the habit of birth control seems to have been of

23

undoubted importance. So far as *motivation* for voluntary limitation is concerned, it may not be altogether irrelevant to note that in this period, when the birth rate was falling, the economy was growing at five to six percent per annum, population was growing by less than one percent per annum (thus per capita incomes were rising substantially), and there was a marked shift in female employment from jobs of low productivity (e.g., domestic service) to those of higher productivity (e.g., industry, commerce, hotels). In such a highly complex issue, one can only conjecture, but the case of Barbados may well indicate that while the two approaches to population control may not succeed if attempts are made to apply them separately, together they stand a good chance of success.

So far as the "politics" of population control is concerned, it seems that this is likely to become a controversial issue in at least two circumstances:

(i) Where a country is split along racial lines, and the two racial groups are roughly of equal size. Advocacy of population control here may well seem like an attempt to prevent the race which has the higher fertility rate from becoming the majority. (This may well be the situation in Guyana, where the people of African descent and the people of East Indian descent are roughly forty percent each of the total population, the other twenty percent being comprised of Chinese and people of European descent.)

(ii) As a result of the Pope's recent pronouncements on birth control, presumably in countries with large Catholic majorities, open advocacy of birth control may cause something even more than a political storm.

We are still far from a solution to the economic problem of a rational distribution of the world's resources amongst all nations and peoples. One source of hope and inspiration as we turn into the last leg of the twentieth century is that there is an awareness of the problem and, among many enlightened countries, many forward-thinking nations and most international institutions, a demonstrated willingness to come to grips with the problem and advise and assist the less fortunate.

Therein perhaps lies salvation. Elsewhere the certainty of extinction.

OVERPOPULATION AND MENTAL HEALTH

George M. Carstairs

George M. Carstairs was born in India in 1916, the son of missionaries of the Church of Scotland. His boyhood was spent in India. On his return to Scotland his education progressed from arts (M.A.) through medicine (M.B., Ch.B.) to psychiatry (M.R.C.P.E., D.P.M.) at the University of Edinburgh, and then to social anthropology at Oxford and New York.

Dr. Carstairs carried out field research in culture and personality in villages of Rajputana, Indian from 1949 to 1952 which was reported in his book "The Twice-Born". From 1953 to 1960 he engaged in research in social psychiatry in Edinburgh. Since 1961 he has been Professor of Psychiatry in Edinburgh University Medical School.

Professor Carstairs has long been a member of the Expert Advisory Panel in Mental Health for the World Health Organization, and has carried out assignments in psychiatry for WHO in a number of countries such as Ceylon, India, Thailand, and Taiwan. He has also visited numerous other countries in Europe, South America, and North America.

He has the distinction of having delivered the BBC Reith Lectures in 1962, titled "This Island Now."

Before I left Edinburgh for Toronto I looked into my office to see if there was anything important in the mail. There wasn't. However, the visit was not entirely wasted because I had the opportunity of picking up the student newspaper. In its centre-page spread I saw a current report on the student scenes where the action was believed to be at its hottest. There were reports from Berkeley, Paris, India, Germany and Toronto. It was in the plane, reading the students' newspaper, that I learned about the interesting district called Yorkville which I gather is the Haight-Ashbury of the Toronto scene.

I have been impressed by the fact that the centres of most vigorous student protest have not been the small private universities. They have been those institutions like Berkeley, and Columbia, and the University of Rome with an enrolment of 70,000, and the Sorbonne with an enrolment of 80,000, and West Berlin. It has always been in extremely large universities that the intense protests have begun. But the protests have only partly been due to the fact that the university student body has increased much more rapidly than has the staff or the teaching facilities. Mere numbers do not trigger protest, but numbers may well have something to do with it.

My main purpose here is not to discuss over-population in the universities but to consider whether rapid increases in world population will have an effect upon mental health. One cannot separate mental health from physical health because if a person is malnourished and sick it is much more difficult to keep a level mind, a level outlook, on the circumstances of his life. We are anxious first of all to know whether we will even be able to feed the increasing population in some parts of the world. Having kept them alive, will we be able to keep them physically healthy? Once that anxiety has been allayed our next consideration concerns the quality of life they are going to lead in new crowded populations.

The first thing we note is that human beings have shown a remarkable capacity for adaptation. Think of the extremes in natural human societies, from north where the Eskimo lives in a tiny community sometimes many days march from the next tiny community, to southern India or Indonesia where landscapes simply teem with humanity in any direction you look. Yet members of both these kinds of community feel at home, feel that this is how one is meant to live, and would be excruciatingly uncomfortable if put in the opposite situation. They have adapted then to a remarkable degree, but at a certain cost—the cost of settling for varying levels of nutrition, of physical hardship, of acceptance of disease. These have been accepted traditionally over many generations because in primitive socièties there has been no awareness that there is any alternative. Indeed there was no other alternative for them until quite recent times. Now this is changing. Almost all people alive now are aware of alternatives. There is a falling death rate, particularly of infants born in such communities, which is seen as a good alternative to high mortality rates.

In former centuries the vast majority of mankind could not indulge in the luxury of aspiring to a high standard of living. Simply to survive into late adulthood, at the same level of subsistence as one's forefathers, was good fortune enough. From the time of the earliest pre-historic civilisations to the present day, in almost every human society, only the privileged elite have been in a position to cultivate their sensibilities, and to expand the boundaries of human experience and understanding. In London, as recently as the beginning of the present century, the very chances of survival through early infancy were more than twice as high for the children of the rich as for the children of the poor. Today, throughout the

26

world, such survival has become more generally attainable for rich and poor alike; and now, for the first time in the history of mankind, education, self-awareness, and the aspiration for a meaningful and satisfying life-experience are being shared to an increasing extent by whole populations.

Inevitably, once the killing diseases and the threat of starvation have been averted, people become increasingly aware of, and discontented with, minor forms of discomfort or unhappiness. One of the striking changes in morbidity, in both highly developed and in developing countries during recent decades has been the apparent increase in neurosis and psycho-somatic disorders. These functional illnesses — which some people would prefer to regard as manifestations of "problems of living" rather than of disease — have long been recognized among the privileged classes. Already in 1689 Thomas Sydenham declared that half of his non-febrile patients (that is, a sixth of his total practice), were hysterical, and in 1733 George Cheyne, in his book entitled "The English Disease," stated that a third of his patients were neurotic. But both Sydenham and Cheyne were fashionable physicians, most of whose clientele was drawn from the wealthy minority of the English society of their day. Sydenham himself observed that hysteria was commoner among women of the leisured classes than among those who had to toil. It is only in the present day that the working classes have been in a position to enjoy the luxury of being neurotic, but recent surveys, both in the East[1] and in the West[2], have shown that already the rates for almost every form of mental illness are highest among the socio-economically under-privileged sections of contemporary societies.

It must be emphasized that the very marked increase in the "visibility" of mental disorders in most countries of the world is partly due to the better control of infections and other serious physical illnesses. Neurosis is a by-product of a raised level of expectation of the quality of life-experience; it can, therefore, act as "divine discontent," a spur towards the further enhancement of the standard of living—provided, of course, that steps *can* be taken to remedy the adverse environmental factors to which the symptoms of neurosis have drawn our attention.

Here we are confronted by a vital question: what will be the consequences, for mental health, of a continuing massive increase in human population?

As yet, the science of human behaviour is not sufficiently developed to be able to answer this question with precision, or even with confidence. Nevertheless it is possible to learn from studies of animals, both in their natural environment and under experimental conditions, and to note certain regularly occurring consequences of severe overcrowding: with due

27

caution, one can infer some similar repercussions of overcrowding in man. There are also a number of direct observations, in human populations, of the interrelationships between overcrowding and certain indices of mental health, from which we can predict with greater confidence the likely consequences of overcrowding on a still larger scale.

Studies of Animal Behaviour

At first sight, it might seem that much could be learned from observations on species such as lemmings, or voles, which are subject to periodic fluctuations of population size. There is still a good deal of controversy among naturalists as to whether these fluctuations are essentially determined by rather gross environmental factors of food supply or infection, or whether social interactions also play an important role. In recent years the work of ethologists has taught us a great deal about the interaction of innate, biological propensities and *learning experiences*, in many animal species. At a relatively crude level, this can be shown in the modification of the animals' adrenal size and activity. The adrenals play an essential role in an animal's response to stress, whether by fighting or by taking flight. There is a conspicuous difference between the size of the adrenals in wild rats and in rats which have been bred for generations in captivity, the latter having much smaller adrenal glands. When wild rats are caged, and allowed to breed, a diminution in adrenal size becomes apparent in a few generations.

In colonies in which there is a great deal of fighting the mean size of the rats' adrenals increases by up to 30 percent—and this is true both of the aggressors and the victims. Observations in nature have shown marked diminution in adrenal size when rat populations are depleted; similar findings have been reported on an overcrowded herd of deer.

Adrenal activity is stimulated by social interaction especially by the challenge of attack and the need for counter-attack in self-defence. It is an interesting finding that the quality of the stress response takes on a different character for the animal which is victorious in the contest. Such an animal can go from strength to strength, able to fight one battle after another and in the intervals of fighting its sexual potency is also at a high level. In contrast, an animal which undergoes a series of defeats becomes debilitated, even although suffering no obvious physical injury, and is sexually less active. The biologist, S. A. Barnett[3] has shown that prolonged exposure to even moderate hostility leads to weakness and death; he has epitomised this reaction as follows: "evidently the bodily response to humiliation resembles, in some ways, that to danger to life or limb." Usually the loser in such contests is able to survive by escaping from the scene of battle and thereafter refraining from challenging its victor; but

28

there are situations both in the wild and in the captive state where animals are unable to escape, and are repeatedly confronted by the threat of a contest in which they are doomed to defeat. Observing such caged rats, Barnett reported that quite often when a rat had been engaged in combat and got the worst of it, that rat would drop dead. Sometimes this happened within hours of when it had been introduced into this threatening environment. Sometimes it happened some days later after prolonged exposure to a succession of threats. Barnett performed post-mortems on the dead rats and found that there was no gross injury, no loss of blood or wounding to account for the sudden death. He did histological studies of their adrenal glands and established to his satisfaction that it was in the first instance due to a massive over-secretion of the medulla of the adrenal gland. In the second instance, it was due to an exhaustion of the cortical cells of the adrenal gland. It seems that exposure to humiliation and defeat can be as physiologically wounding in its way as actual physical trauma.

An analogy may be found in observations on the toxicity of amphetamine drugs, whose action is similar to that of adrenaline, the secretion of the medulla of the adrenal gland. A relatively small dose of amphetamine will prove fatal to a rat which is confined in a cage with many other rats, whereas a rat which is kept in isolation can survive doses of amphetamine up to four times greater. It is presumed that the effect of the drug is greatly enhanced, in the former situation, by the numerous stressful interactions with the other rats, each of which stimulates the output of more adrenaline until complete exhaustion supervenes.

These, of course, represent extremes of over-stimulation. Many species of animals and birds have evolved self-protective behaviour patterns to ensure that such extremes will not occur. Typical of these behaviour patterns is the "peck order" or status hierarchy, by virtue of which a group of animals who meet each other regularly first fight each other, and then mutually agree on a rank-order of ascendancy after which the animal of inferior status invariably concedes in the face of a challenge from those above him in rank. More detailed studies[4,5] have shown that status hierarchies can be either *absolute*, where every member of a group of animals invariably remains in the same position in relation to each of his fellows, or *relative* in which, under different circumstances of time or place, the individual's respective degrees of ascendancy over each other may change. Absolute status heirarchy is most likely to be found where all the animals in a group share the same living-space, and it becomes most clearly defined when that space is a restricted one. Under such circumstances, Barnett has shown that adrenal size becomes inversely correlated with height in the social hierarchy.

Relative dominance is seen most clearly in animals which have individual territories. When on their home ground, they are often able to vanquish an intruder and compel him to retreat, whereas if they are challenged by the same individual on *his* home territory they in turn will admit defeat. It seems that not only birds, but most mammals (including man) exhibit this kind of territorial behaviour. Not only football teams, but all of us, tend to perform best on our home ground—mental as well as physical—and to resist anyone who ventures to challenge us there. Naturalists have recognized in territorial behaviour, and in the varying degrees of dominance associated with the centre and the periphery of the territory, a self-regulating mechanism which ensures an optimal degree of dispersion of the species. It has also been noted that if several rats are introduced at the same time into a strange environment they coexist amicably; but if strangers are subsequently added they fight the stranger.

When animals such as domestic cats, which customarily enjoy quite a wide range of movement, are crowded together in a limited space there tends to emerge one particularly tyrannical "despot" who holds all the others in fear, and also one or more whom Leyhausen[6] terms "pariahs," at the bottom of the status hierarchy. These unfortunate creatures, he observes, are "driven to frenzy and all kinds of neurotic behaviour by continuous and pitiless attack by all the others." Although these "pariahs" bear the severest brunt, the whole community of cats held in such close confinement is seen to suffer. These cats "seldom relax, they never look at ease, and there is continuous hissing, growling and even fighting. Play stops altogether, and locomotion and exercise are reduced to a minimum." *(Ibid.)*

This clearly represents a pathological social situation, in which overcrowding and confinement conspire to accentuate disturbing confrontations between individuals. In Hamburg some years ago the rats became a plague to such a point that a special campaign had to be mounted in the sewers of the city. Biologists took advantage of this experiment of nature to study the rats before and after the extermination campaign. The campaign actually reduced their numbers to something like one-tenth of what they had been at the height of the plague. It was noticed that weight for weight there was a very significant reduction in the size of the adrenal glands when the numbers of the rat population were diminished by the extermination programme. A precisely similar finding was reported by another naturalist who studied a herd of deer which increased in numbers till it was over-populating its territory and then had to be artificially reduced. Again there was an increase in the size of the adrenal with the increase in population, and a diminution when the numbers in the territory were reduced.

A comparative psychologist, John Calhoun,[7] studying the behaviour of colonies of rats under different degrees of over-population observed similar changes in their customary inter-relationships. Where overcrowding was most marked, the enforced social interactions were seen to interfere with the satisfaction of quite basic biological needs such as feeding, nest-building and the care of their young. Normally mother rats whose nest is disturbed will carry their young one by one to a place of safety, but in overcrowded pens this behaviour pattern was lost, and the rat's maternal care became so faulty that in one experiment 80 percent and in another 96 percent of all the young died before reaching maturity. Among the males, some became ascendant over their fellows but others showed a number of disturbances of behaviour, of which two patterns were particularly striking: some males appeared to opt out of sexual and social interaction altogether, skulking alone on the periphery of the group, while others became morbidly hypersexual, mounting female rats, whether receptive or not, whenever they could do so without being attacked by one of the ascendant males. The latter type of action is very unusual among wild mammals. These hyperactive rats contravened many of the norms of behaviour of their group, even becoming cannibal towards the young of their own kind. Christian, observing mice, showed that with overcrowding the reproduction rate is lowered: there are stillbirths and failure of lactation, and hence infant deaths. There is also a delayed effect; the next generation shows faulty maternal behaviour.

These observations on rats and cats must be regarded as having only marginal relevance to human experience and human behaviour. We come a little nearer the human when we read of studies carried out by biologists on primates. For many years, in fact from 1932 till almost 1965, an old text of Zuckerman's[8] was the chief authority on primate behaviour. (It is alleged that a London bookseller advertised it as dealing with the sex life of bishops.) It was the report of very careful observations on primate behaviour carried out in a succession of extended visits to zoos in South Africa where he observed baboons and chimpanzees in captivity. He pictured their behaviour as being dominated by competition, particularly competition for sexual dominance within the little group, and fighting. It is only in quite recent years that Schaller, Washburn, De Vore,[9] Jane Goodall and other ethologists have reported on how these species behave in their natural wild state. We now realize that accurate though Zuckerman's observations were, they reflected a totally distorted picture of the natural behaviour of these apes. It was a picture of the behaviour of apes confined in a space much more crowded than their natural habitat. Even gorillas seem to engage in a very few combats and relatively few threatening behaviourisms in their natural state. On the other hand

31

observations on packs of monkeys in India which inhabit the fringe of jungles near human villages indicate an increase in the frequency of combative encounters as the packs increase in size.

Observations on Humans

What about human behaviour in confined conditions? We do have some direct reports from survivors of concentration camps among whom are the outstanding psychologist Bettelheim[10] of Chicago, and the psychiatrist Eitinger[11] of Norway. Their candid reports of what it is like to be in a concentration camp with an extreme improbability of coming out alive make rather bitter reading because they show how even the most upright and courageous people tended to show a deterioration in their usual humanitarian values. It was exceptionally rare for anyone to be able to maintain his standards under these extreme conditions.

Others have described conditions of life in the slightly less rigorous but still very crowded and confined conditions of prisoner-of-war camps. Two biologists who have shown a special interest in this field have been Paul Leyhausen[6] and Konrad Lorenz, both of whom endured several years of internment in prisoner-of-war camps. Lorenz, who writes with such marvellous eloquence, has described his own experiences in a Russian prisoner-of-war camp. He tells very candidly how, after a longish confinement, he found the slightest mannerisms of his companions in the officers' huts to be unendurably irritating. However, he had the presence of mind to recognize the irrationality of his bad temper and when he found himself seething he would leave the company of his companions, walk to the barbed wire and look out across the acres of snow and empty land until his temperature subsided and he was fit to rejoin his fellows. The experiences of Leyhausen and Lorenz have been corroborated by other medical and psychiatric witnesses.[10,12,13]

These too, like the observations on caged cats and rats, were instances of extreme conditions, and yet one has to realize that there are many impoverished groups in the world whose conditions of life today are scarcely better. In theory, of course, they can escape from their surroundings, but in practice the "culture of poverty" can induce a sense of despair of ever being able to escape.[14] One is tempted to draw an analogy between the rat which is subjected to a series of physical defeats, or the "pariahs" in an overcrowded colony of cats, and the members of problem families in our city slums who display a seeming inability to make a successful social adaptation. It appears that social institutions and transmitted value systems can create a sense of confinement no less demoralizing than the bars of a cage. People can be confined just as effectively by growing up in an impoverished social milieu as they can by iron bars. There is a sense of incapability to escape when one has been denied the opportunity to develop one's intellectual faculties, to develop the imagination, to develop skills or capacities which would enable one to break away from these belittling surroundings.

Many years ago, Faris and Dunham[15] drew attention to the ecological concentration of certain forms of mental illness in those parts of a large city where both overcrowding and social disorganization—or *anomie* as Durkheim[16] had earlier described it—were most marked. Subsequent research has challenged Dunham's specific contention that schizophrenia is generated by the conditions of life in a socially disorganized community, but many other studies have confirmed his demonstration that alcoholism, illegitimacy, divorce, delinquency, and numerous other forms of social pathology are most prevalent in such areas.

There remains, however, an interesting contrast, in the social correlates of two particular manifestations of social pathology, namely *suicide* and *attempted suicide*, at least as they are observed in cities of the Western world. Suicide rates are highest in areas where many people live in a state of *social isolation*, bereft of the support family, or of any other primary group. On the other hand studies of attempted suicide have shown that the most important social correlate is *overcrowding*. Typically, the person who makes a non-fatal suicidal gesture has been harassed beyond endurance by recurrent friction within the domestic group, in cramped and overcrowded premises. Here too, as in the instance of rats' dose-resistance to amphetamine, one can see the mutual reinforcement of multiple factors. A majority of those who attempt suicide are relatively young men and women, who often have had a bad start in life with unstable or absent parent-figures. These patients tend to experience great difficulty in their turn, in forming stable inter-personal relationships; they are often at the same time demanding and inconsiderate towards others, and yet themselves emotionally immature and dependent. Their deficiencies prompt them to seek out partners from whom they hope to derive support, but all too often the partner whom they select is handicapped in much the same way; so far from meeting each other's dependency needs, these unfortunates only succeed in making each other's state even worse than before. Often, too, they turn to drink or drugs to allay their need for dependence and this in turn further impoverishes their ability to form rewarding personal relationships.[17] During recent years many countries have been obliged to take stock of increasing rates of alcoholism, delinquency and attempted suicide, indicating that an increasing number of citizens in our large cities feel alienated from the goals and the rewards to which their fellow citizens aspire, and alienated so profoundly that they despair of every being able to get back into the mainstream of humanity.

Alienation and despair are the product of extreme situations, such as those, as I have noted, that were realized in the grotesque, doomed societies of the Nazi concentration camps. Many, if not most, of the inmates of such camps found themselves surrendering their customary standards of behaviour and their values, becoming completely disoriented by the inhuman conditions under which they were forced to live.[11]

There have been crises, in the course of human history, when quite large sectors of mankind experienced this sense of alienation from participation in the life of their fellow-countrymen. Sometimes after prolonged deprivation their discontents have exploded in outbreaks of revolution, as a result of which a new social order has been created; but at other times leaderless masses of the dispossessed have shown themselves only too ready to become the dupes of mentally unstable yet charismatic demagogues, who promised them a magical deliverance from their miseries. As Norman Cohn[18] shows, they become the leaders of milllennial cults, promising the dawn of a golden age. An interesting thing about these milllennial cults, which have recurred over and over again in European history, is that they begin with a preaching of brotherhood, generosity, sharing, saying that the riches of the earth are going to be shared among us all. It is a naive Utopian optimism. They waited for a magical answer to all their problems, and of course the magical answer was denied, the dream remained unfulfilled.

Indeed quite soon the authorities, the Establishment of the day, began to take repressive measures against the dupes of these demagogic leaders, and then came a clash. The repressive forces were seen as hostile, threatening, demoniacal, and the movement which began with brotherhood, peace and charity, inevitably ended in bloodshed, and sometimes in extremely violent bloodshed. One sees this story repeated over and over again.

Such an incident, though in a new guise, occurred after the Second World War. "Cargo cults" emerged in the islands of Polynesia and Indonesia. Cargo cults are rather like the milllennial movements of the Middle Ages in Europe. There was a preaching of a magical solution to the problems of the poor and underprivileged. The name derived from the belief that a cargo airplane was going to land and pour out a cornucopia of all the things that they had witnessed with the sudden intrusion of Western troops. Jeeps, radios, washing machines were going to be delivered in abundance. These cults began with kindliness, naive hopes and innocent expectations, and ended with frustration, anger and bloodshed.

A similar phenomenon has occurred repeatedly in modern times, when the pace of political change has out-stripped a society's capacity to meet the newly aroused expectations of its members. When, because of increasing overpopulation, the standards of living actually decline at the very time when people's aspirations have been raised, the stage is set for further outbreaks of collective irrationality and violence.[19] This is the predicament of many developing areas today: India, Indonesia, South America, West Africa.

Now, going back to the beginning of my talk, I remind you that many of the movements of student protest in recent years have also begun generously, with concepts of brotherhood and concern for their fellow men. And this is still true of large elements in them. It is true of the work that many American students have done to further the cause of integration. It is true of the impulse that led them to protest against the war in Vietnam. For quite a time it was maintained in this style. They talked of flower power and of love-ins, feeling that this generous spirit would prevail and would be recognized and accepted. There is just a hint now, perhaps especially since the unhappy events of the Chicago Convention, that there has been a turn in this milennial movement. I notice, consulting the student newspaper from Edinburgh, that in certain quarters the slogan of "Flower Power" is being replaced by a new ugly slogan, "Kill the pig." You can see the sequence. The repressive forces, the men in blue with truncheons, have appeared and are now being portrayed by some as the forces of evil, an exaggerated, demoniacal, bad object whom it is permitted to hate. And I think we have to be on our guard against this.

It is not numbers only, it is in addition the crash of high expectations frustrated. This gives rise to anger and, if we don't look out, to violence and bloodshed. In that sequence, I suggest, is the real threat of uncontrolled overpopulation to mental health. It is imperative that we recognize the gravity of this threat, because mankind today possesses weapons of such destructive power that the world cannot afford to risk outbreaks of mass violence; and yet the lesson of history points to just such a disaster, unless population control can be achieved before vast human communities degenerate into the semblance of concentration camp inmates, if not to that of Zuckerman's pathologically belligerent apes.

1. — Lin, T.Y. (1953). A study of the incidence of mental disorder in Chinese and other cultures. *Psychiatry, 16,* 313.

2. — Srole, L., Langner, T.S., Michael, S.T., Opler, M.K. and Rennie, T.A.C. (1962). *Mental Health in the Metropolis.* New York: McGraw Hill.

3. — Barnett, S.A. (1964). The biology of agression. *Lancet,* ii, 803.

4. — Wynne-Edwards, V.C. (1962). *Animal Dispersion in Relation to Social Behaviour.* Edinburgh and London: Oliver and Boyd.

5. – Leyhausen, P. (1965a). The communal organisation of solitary mammals. *Sym. Roy. Soc. Lond., 14,* 249.

6. – Leyhausen, P. (1965b). The sane community – a density problem? *Discovery*, September 1965.

7. – Calhoun, J.B. (1963). Population density and social pathology. (In: Duhl, L.J. *The Urban Condition.* New York: Basic Books).

8. – Zuckerman, P.G. (1932). *The Social Life of Monkeys and Apes.* London: Kegan Paul.

9. – De Vore, I. (1965). *Primate Behaviour.* New York: Treubner King.

10. – Bettelheim, B. (1963). Individual and mass behaviour in extreme situations. *J. Abnormal and Soc. Psychol., 58,* 417.

11. – Eitinger, L. (1961). *Concentration Camp Survivors in Norway and Israel.* Allen and Unwin.

12. – Cochrane, A.L. (1946). Notes on the psychology of prisoners of war. *Brit. Med. J., i,* 282.

13. – Gibbens, T.C.N. (1947). *The Psychology and Psychopathology of the Prisoners of War.* M.D. thesis, University of London.

14. – Lewis, Oscar. (1959). *Five Families: Mexican Case Studies in the Culture of Poverty.* New York: Basic Books.

15. – Faris, R.E.L. and Dunham, H.W. (1939). *Mental Disorders in Urban Areas.* Chicago University Press.

16. – Durkheim, E. (1897). *Le Suicide.* Paris.

17. – Kessel, W.I.N. and McCulloch, J.W. (1966). Repeated Acts of Self-Poisoning and Self-Injury. *Proc. Roy. Soc. Med., 59,* 89.

18. – Cohn, N. (1957). *The Pursuit of the Millenium.* London: Secher and Warburg.

19. – Worsley, P. (1957). *The Trumpet Shall Sound.* London: MacGibbon and Kee.

DISCUSSION FOLLOWING

FIRST SESSION

Fr. Baum:

I would ask Mr. Barrow, the Prime Minister of Barbados, to say a few words specifically about the problems of his country. I realize that a Prime Minister may not wish to talk about his problems to other people outside his country and if this were a political gathering I wouldn't ask. But this is, after all, a Teach-In and I thought you might share with us how your own people respond to the programs of population control. In particular, how does the problem of the conflict of races affect the population problems in your country?

Mr. Barrow:

The first problem in Barbados at the moment, as in most of the developing countries, is the problem of finding jobs for the people who are already there. We are not particularly worried about the dynamics of population in Barbados because we have stabilized our growth rates. We have considerably increased the rate of growth of our gross domestic product as I explained in my brief talk. But we are one of the primary producing countries in the world and we feel that we could considerably improve our standard of living if we were to get better prices for our primary products. So our problem is not one of controlling the rate of population growth. We do not consider that we are overpopulated in the absolute sense of the term. We have a much higher standard of living than 75 percent of the nations which are represented in the United Nations Organization. Our problem is how to convince the larger developed countries with whom we have been traditionally associated by trade and by history to pay us better prices for our products.

Fr. Baum:

If one set of technological processes produces all kinds of unhappy consequences, why can't we find other processes which produce more happy ones? Dr. Cole, do you think that it would be possible to develop our technology in such a way that these unfortunate by-products will

37

become less and less?

Dr. Cole:

This is another economic problem, simply a matter of dollars and cents for the most part. Factories do not have to put sulphur dioxide into the atmosphere; they can convert it into a valuable commercial product—sulphuric acid. This is also true of nitrogen oxides, which can be converted into nitric acid. But these acids are not now valuable enough to induce factory managers to make the change-over.

One major gasoline manufacturer is putting out a lead-free high-test gasoline at a price no higher than the leaded products of competitors. (Lead poisons the particular catalyst which is the basis for some of the methods proposed to rid motor vehicle exhausts of other harmful components.) The competitors scream with anguish because it would cost them a lot to change to the new type of refinery that would make lead-free gasoline production practical. I don't think they are going to make the change until somebody tells them they have to.

Nuclear power plants do not have to release radioactive materials into the atmosphere or into their cooling water. They do it because it would cost them an unspecified amount of money not to. Automobile bodies have value, and if civilization goes on long enough old junk yards are surely going to become mines. It simply is not economically feasible now to force people to reclaim these things and recycle them.

Garbage by and large can be converted into fertilizer, or it can be burned as is being done in plants in Europe. It can be burned in such a way that the resulting ashes become valuable building materials, but again these are not economically competitive methods except under special conditions. Yes, technology can go a long way towards solving these problems, but it can't solve them all; if we don't stop population growth the other problems are insoluble.

The U.S. Secretary of the Interior, Mr. Udall, recently commented that the aluminum beer can is a disaster. It will be there shining in the sun a hundred years from now. Technology is producing these new things that won't recycle. At least the old iron can eventually did rust. There is encouragement on this scene though because there has recently been patented in the Netherlands a plastic container that is very stable as long as it's full. When it is empty is breaks down very rapidly and disappears. This may be one of history's great inventions provided that the substances it breaks down into are harmless. I don't know what they are.

Fr. Baum:

Dr. Carstairs has warned us of seeking magical solutions for our great

38

problems and has warned against a sense of over urgency and false expectation and disappointment. Also he has talked about the psychological problems created by living close together, and about the adaptability of man.

It occurs to me that there is a necessity today to introduce basic therapeutic methods to our society, that is, to make a therapeutic society. Is it possible to introduce basic therapeutic principles in our schools in the way that we teach hygienic principles, for example? Are there some therapeutic principles which could be communicated at an early level in schools so that persons will be able to deal with some of the crises that arise through close living, and the problems that arise from unrealistic expectations, and so on?

Dr. Carstairs:

One would like to think that the answer is yes. There is certainly no simple answer. One of the hopeful things today is that people are increasingly becoming aware of destructive and negative aspects of our society; in fact, to my mind this is the real undercurrent to the student protest that is breaking out in so many countries all over the world. It is due to an awareness of negative aspects of the societies for which they are being prepared, and they are not willing simply to accept an adult society which they find wanting. The next stage of course is deciding how to change that society and into what it should be changed. I mentioned the cargo cults as having failed because they relied on magic, but in fact there are instances where a primitive society came into the twentieth century on rational terms. They had the good fortune to have a leader who was not a half-crazed demagogue but was a man with a modest degree of education, enough to know that you have to have a basic knowledge, a simple knowledge, and a basic technology before you can get the rewards of the better-off countries in the world. He persuaded his fellows in his group that the way to improve their lot was to gain that basic education and training which was the secret behind the western people's higher standard of material existence. This was the alternative rational approach.

I think there is still scope for indoctrination of the rational approach in our young, even if this sometimes challenges some of the religious instruction they are given. I think some of our schools' religious instruction carries with it an unhappy continuation of simple indoctrination of mythology and legend, backed with the pretext of faith. But there are other traditions in your own church, Father Baum, which welcome intellectual enquiry and use faith simply to fill in the gap of the ultimate limits of human knowledge. So I would say increase the rational sceptical enquiring preparation of young people, even at the cost of protest, when they get older. Even more important I think is emotional preparation, but that would take me on to a rather long divergence on the emotional settings in which people display social pathology and request treatment by psychiatrists in their later life.

Questioner:

Dr. Cole referred to the danger to human survival caused by the destruction of rain forests in tropical countries by industrialization. Yet without technological development it may be very difficult to raise the people there above the poverty level. How would he propose that we resolve this difficulty?

Dr. Cole:

They have to decide how large a population can actually be supported in those countries without this destruction and then operate in such a way as to keep the population within the tolerable limit. Better use can be made of these rain forests than is being made today without destroying them. There are possibilities for harvesting the native animals rather than trying to replace them. It would probably be considerably more efficient. to utilize the renewable resources of the African tropical forests than to replace them with conventional agricultural crops and cattle. Tropical soils are such that if you go in and try to develop an area where a tropical rain forest is growing, you may wind up with a soil that not only is the colour of brick but is also as hard as brick and useful only for building materials. Certainly this is not the way to develop a higher standard of living in a country.

Questioner:

Dr. Carstairs, do you think that we in Canada should worry about an exploding Canadian population, or should we be more concerned with assisting other people to solve their more acute problems?

Dr. Carstairs:

I believe that you have still got a certain amount of room in Canada. But I entirely take your point that it doesn't absolve you from being concerned with other parts of the world whose problems are acute. It is one of the remarkable things about the period since the Second World War, how much more real has become our awareness of problems all over the world. I endorse your feeling that even if Canada hasn't a problem on its doorstep it is entitled to be concerned for our fellows in other parts of the world.

Questioner:

Dr. Cole, why are some of your chemically knowledgeable colleagues interested in interrupting the nitrogen cycle? Secondly, in view of the rather horrifying picture you present to us, what measures do you think will be instituted by the American government within the next decade that will help to combat some of the pollution that is presently occurring?

Dr. Cole:

In reply to the first question, they want to interfere with the nitrogen cycle by getting rid of the so-called de-nitrifiers which convert nitrate back into molecular nitrogen. Their concern is with agricultural efficiency. They think it's a dirty trick: first we put all this nitrate fertilizer on the soil and our poor little bacteria helpers in the roots of legumes work so hard fixing molecular nitrogen in the form of nitrate; then these other vicious de-nitrifying organisms come along and undo the process. But our efficiency experts simply don't realize that the integrity of the atmosphere depends on having denitrification going on just as rapidly as nitrogen fixation is occurring.

Concerning the second question, I am a little more optimistic now that I was perhaps a year ago. Delegations, largely from the Ecological Society of America, have been talking with members of Congress. At first for the most part they merely listened politely. Now they are starting to listen actively. They have recently formed an ad hoc committee, both House and Senate, to learn about the environment and have invited a number of us to serve as scientific advisors to them. My latest information is that one hundred members of the House of Representatives had joined this body. I find it very encouraging that people who are in the position to make decisions are at least becoming concerned and starting to listen. Now I hesitate to say how much this will accomplish in ten years. Hopefully the problem will be understood by that time, because it looks to those of us who tried to draw up the balance sheet that we are in for a world food crisis probably within ten to 15 years. Dr. Borgstrom can give you more reliable figures on this subject than I could. Of course, when the disaster actually hits, then everyone will be willing to do something.

Questioner:

Dr. Carstairs gave several examples from animal behaviour, and it would seem that magnitude in numbers leads to social disorder, tension, and lack of harmony. How does he explain the fact that the number of mental cases in the western world by far surpasses the mental cases in the Asian countries.

41

Dr. Carstairs:

Before I explain it you would have to convince me that the number of mental cases in the western world far surpasses those in the Asian countries. I just don't believe it. Only one really thorough survey has been carried out in the Asian countries and that was done on Chinese populations. The conclusion was that serious mental illness was to be found in those populations at just the same rate as in Northern Europe. Perhaps the minor mental disorders, neuroses, psychosomatic disorders, which we have lumped in with what we call the diseases of civilization, perhaps these do occur at a higher rate in Europe. We don't have accurate counts in the West or in the East, but at least I would be prepared to entertain the likelihood that they are more frequent in highly developed societies with a rapid pace of daily life.

Questioner:

Dr. Carstairs, do you think that reactions of aggression and intolerance are innate?

Dr. Carstairs:

At least the propensity to anger is innate in all of us. Don't we know it! Part of healthy living in communities means somehow containing the potentially destructive elements in our nature so that they won't be destructive, either to others or to ourselves.

Perhaps I have neglected to point out that crowding doesn't always result in violence to others. In my own researches I have been specially interested in the incidence of suicide and attempted suicide. Attempted suicide in particular has overcrowding as a high social correlate. It is a phenomenon of people getting on each other's nerves in overcrowded conditions, in complete contrast to actual suicide which is a phenomenon above all of loneliness.

Dr. Cole:

Speaking as a zoologist there is always at least a slight risk in generalizing from another kind of animal to man. Dr. Carstairs gave us a good description of the stress syndrome which arises in rats as a result of crowding, but we could pick close relatives of the rats that behave somewhat differently. One extreme is the muskrat. Muskrat populations don't get overcrowded. If the marsh starts to dry up, leading to crowding, strife breaks out that drives away part of the population and brings it down to the level that can be supported. There is great wisdom in this.

At the other end of the spectrum is the house mouse. In the late 1920's when an outbreak of house mice occurred near Bakersfield,

California, one of the world's leading mammalogists happened to be on the scene and made surveys of the numbers of mice that were involved. The average came, as I recall, to 18.4 mice per square yard, over 84,000 per acre. You literally couldn't step without walking on mice. They of course destroyed the environment and then perished from starvation. There was no chance for the environment to support populations of that magnitude.

Now it may be a little more hopeful if man is more like the rat. He is certainly not as wise as the muskrat, and I am afraid he may be a little bit more like the mouse.

Questioner:

Dr. Cole suggested reversing the trend to overpopulation and decreasing the population. How could this be done?

Dr. Cole:

Simply by bringing down the birthrates. We have the technology to do this in a variety of ways at the present time. I am not suggesting going out and killing anyone or anything of that sort, but natural attrition will bring the population down quite rapidly if we bring the world birthrate down below about 15 per 1,000.

Mr. Barrow:

I would like to take up Dr. Cole on one of the points which he made earlier. I cannot accept his concepts of not clearing away the rain forests. Let me give you an illustration of what can happen. In Guyana the aluminum industry is controlled by Canadian capital. To get at the bauxite, the raw material of aluminum, the rain forest must be removed. This contributes far more to the national economy than leaving the country in rain forests.

What I don't like about Dr. Cole's thesis on this particular point – I don't mean to take issue with his address in general – is that it appears to me to condemn the underdeveloped countries to do their duty in that state of life to which it has pleased the Almighty to call them and to remain in this state of underdevelopment with the very picturesque tropical rain forests when underneath the rain forests there may be unlimited mineral and other resources which can raise the living standards of the countries.

Dr. Cole:

I didn't mean to imply that rain forests are sacred above any other type of natural community. I am sure we would dispense with our cornfields if somebody found gold underneath them.

Fr. Baum:

I have a question here from somebody who may be a little shy because of the density of the population in this hall. Does Dr. Carstairs think that there is a relationship between the rising level of violence in the United States and the overcrowding in the cities?

Dr. Carstairs:

What do *you* think? Quite seriously isn't one of the astonishing things of the year that has just passed the fact that there has been so little violence in the U.S.A. After 1967 we were expecting extremes of violence, and 1968 began so badly with the murder of Martin Luther King, the murder of Bobby Kennedy. We on the other side of the Atlantic thought that this was going to be the year of the holocaust. Perhaps it is going to be next year.

But quite truly I don't think it is overcrowding in itself. I think instead that it is what is behind that overcrowding that is the problem. It is the inequality, particularly glaring in the case of the coloured people in the population of the U.S.A. We are seeing in the American colour confrontation just what we are seeing in other parts of the world. I think Mr. Barrow would agree with me that people are suddenly waking up, looking. Dr. Sukarno of Indonesia, now in a state of eclipse, put it very vividly some years ago. He said the movies can be a revolutionary agent because a person with a very meagre standard of living sees working men in other countries driving an automobile. He sees working men owning refrigerators and washing machines and to see that can excite a spirit of revolt. People have an awareness of things that they are missing and have a growing determination that they are not going to put up with deprivation any longer. That, I think, is the seed of impatience and violence not only in the U.S.A. but in other parts of the world too.

Mr. Barrow:

I would like to emphasize that we have to discard a lot of the popular concepts of population densities which we read about in textbooks and in the newspapers. To talk about so many people per square mile is not really a valid concept in the twentieth century. It would be appropriate only if all other things were equal and each country was producing for one square mile exactly what the other country was producing. It is far more realistic to look at all the factors which integrate in creating the domestic product of a country. The old-time concepts seem to imply that people in Barbados with a population density of 1,400 per square mile are much more badly off than people in the Sahara who have 1,400 square miles per person. Everybody knows that that is false.

Questioner:

Dr. Cole, if a serious attempt were made now, say on the level of the American space program, to de-pollute our environment, what progress could we expect? Could it be returned to a stable state or to the original state?

Dr. Cole:

I am sure the 5 billion dollar annual budget of NASA would be far too small to do this. It would take a large program to rehabilitate Lake Erie, much less the entire environment of the world. We could of course reduce a great deal of the pollution. We could start the process of bringing the population to a level at which it can be supported with a decent standard of living. Hopefully we can eventually bring the world environment into a stable condition where it would not continue to deteriorate.

We "know" that the world can support some unknown number of people indefinitely at a respectable standard of living. We are of course assuming optimistically that we haven't already done something that makes our continued existence untenable. There are a few alarming little things that a recent study in Long Island Sound has shown. DDT is actually depressing very gradually the rate of green plant photosynthesis. We are continuing to add DDT to the oceans. There may be other materials that are operating this way too.

Some geneticists are worried about the genetic load, the load of defective genes that have already been imposed on the population but won't begin to appear until future generations. There is no way of telling how many of these there are; it is conceivable that we may already have exterminated ourselves, but I don't know anyone who considers this probable. It is an extremely frightening and difficult question and it certainly should be in our minds when we permit any further contamination of the environment with things that are capable of producing genetic changes.

Questioner:

Dr. Carstairs, in your studies in India where adaptation for population density has apparently occurred, did you observe any value changes or personality deficiencies?

Dr. Carstairs:

This year I paid a short visit to the first village I lived in, and it has changed astonishingly little, in 18 years. They were celebrating building the first house in the village that wasn't of mud and stone—there was some cement in it—but they still have to draw water from the well, still have an extremely rudimentary standard of living. Their biggest change is in communications. There is now a hard road passing near the village with buses running on it. India is a country with such an enormous mass and such an enormous population mass that it takes a long time to get that mass in motion. Once it gets going it might start going with a rush but in my brief span I can say that in village life in India I have not seen it going with a rush. In the enormous cities it is a different story and not entirely a cheerful one. I recall that the first psychiatric clinic in the big teaching hospital in Bombay in 1949 had two hundred patients throughout the year. When I called on them in 1964 they had six thousand new patients in the year. This doesn't mean that there were new cases or a higher incidence of psychiatric illness. I think it rather meant that their service was getting known and reaching many more of that enormous population.

Questioner:

Dr. Carstairs dwelt upon some of the human problems in the population explosion. Do we really pay much attention to the humanistic part of the problem? It seems that in this Teach-In and in many other analyses we are so concerned about the physical aspects, the contraceptive devices, the ecology, the methods of producing more food for the numbers of people. It seems we are stressing exploding humanity but we are forgetting about the humanity part and talking about exploding bodies.

Dr. Carstairs:

I think you are perfectly right, numbers are not the whole story. It's the significance behind the numbers to which we ought to address ourselves.

SECOND SESSION

SEEING INTO THE PRESENT

STATUS OF WOMEN AND FAMILY PLANNING
IN A DEVELOPING COUNTRY—EGYPT

Mrs. Aziza Hussein

Mrs. Aziza Hussein makes her home in Cairo, United Arab Republic. A leading feminist, she worked for years in the cause of women's status in Arab countries and the closely related problems of family planning and birth control.

Mrs. Hussein is a Founder of the Egyptian Family Planning Association. She has been a delegate of the UAR to the UN Commission on Human Rights, the UN Mission to Pakistan, the UN Commission on the Status of Women and other UN committees. She has participated in other important international conferences, such as the 1967 Santiago conference of the International Planned Parenthood Federation.

Her publications include such titles as "The Role of Women in Social Reform in Egypt" in 1953, "Status of Women in Family Law in the U.A.R." in 1964, and "Changing Conditions of Women and its Effect on Children" in 1966.

Theoretically the practice of family planning has a direct bearing on the status of women in society, and vice versa, for the following reasons:

1. People concerned with the status of women in present-day society have related the subordinate status imposed on women throughout the ages in most civilizations to *physiological* differences between men and women. These differences made woman depend on man for protection of her and her children, and also dictated the way that community tasks should be divided between her and her husband. As such she was a follower and a second to man, her protector. Laws and institutions were further established which more firmly entrenched the woman in this one-sided more or less biological role. Man's effort to provide for his family gradually involved him in diversified occupations which developed his mental and artistic faculties, whereas the woman was limited in her capacity to grow and develop as an intelligent being, as a result of which she came to be regarded as mentally inferior to man.

2. High mortality in the past, resulting from various hazards, epidemics, wars, famines, the unavailability of medical care, etc., was

responsible for human society always having a stake in the maintenance of its numbers and in sanctions, sometimes severe, against measures which threatened to curb procreation. This fact by itself served to emphasize the species preservative role of women. However women always found ways of controlling their unwanted pregnancies, and the most widely used means was induced abortions at the risk of health and life. Illegal abortion is probably the most common crime that has been committed by women for long centuries, and for which severe penalties have been paid. The death sentence was inflicted on abortionists in France as recently as 1943.[1]

3. Besides exposing women to the dangers of induced abortions, uncontrolled and excessive childbearing has undesirable repercussions on the physical, mental and moral well-being, which are now well recognized and which are by no means shared by her male partner. For example, with respect to the health of the mother, it has been medically recognized that "the timing of pregnancies, the interval between them, the number of pregnancies·a mother has during the span of her childbearing years, have important consequences for the survival, health and well-being of mother and offspring."[2]

4. In view of the foregoing considerations, the practice of family planning by contraceptive means becomes a woman's human right. By making it possible for the woman to choose the time of conception and the size of her family, it enables her not only to protect her health and perhaps to save her life, but also to maintain her status as a person instead of being a biological tool—a person who should be able to plan her life and shape her destiny, and have the opportunity to develop her talents and to advance, and also to contribute to the cultural and economic life of her society.

5. As parenthood becomes voluntary, not only are women delivered from the biological servitude of unplanned pregnancies, but, in the words of a sociologist, "children come to be wanted more consciously as expressions of the creative and affection giving potentialities of their parents." Experience has demonstrated, moreover, that the practice of family planning as an expression of responsible parenthood is associated with higher standards of education in general, and with the higher status of women in education and employment in particular.

6. With the population explosion posing a new kind of threat to humanity, conception control becomes even more important as an urgent social necessity.

7. Taking another angle on the status of women, that which is related to sexual morality, contraception serves, in the view of some modern thinkers, another important purpose. Because illegitimacy has

always been considered a threat to the family, the fundamental unit of society, a heavier burden of moral responsibility has been placed in most societies on women than on men, married or unmarried. The double standard of morality, in many societies, and the discrimination against women in many penal codes in matters of sexual offences, are but expressions of a social injustice perpetrated by the fear of illegitimacy. Contraception is considered a means which eventually helps to promote equal moral responsibility between men and women, inside and outside the family. The dissociation of the procreative function from sexual activity by means of contraception helps to remove the penalty which is unilaterally attached to the woman's sexual behaviour. While I am far from being a proponent of sexual freedom for either men or women, it is my belief that moral behaviour should not be motivated by fear of conception or social stigma, but by conviction and free choice. So why not give men and women an equal chance?

8. There is yet another relationship which could be established between excessive population growth and the lower status of women. Not only do women share the problems created by overpopulation with the other sex, but they suffer from their own special problems as well. In the case of unemployment or scarcity of educational facilities, it is the women who are expendable, for after all men are still the traditional breadwinners in most societies, particularly in developing countries. Furthermore special services for women, such as medical facilities in maternal and child health centres, are likely to become inadequate when the expansion of such facilities is not able to cope with the growing number of women who need them.

To my knowledge family planning, as a means of liberating women from old time biological servitude, has not figured on the agendas of feminist rallies or women's meetings until very recently, when the urgency of the population explosion has brought about a change of attitude. There is no doubt that the controversial nature of birth control, with the taboos attending the subject of sex, has delayed the frank discussion of this vital issue too long, while women all over the world have resorted to secretly induced abortions. And when the subject was discussed for the first time in an international women's gathering (The International Council of Women in 1963), it was handled with caution within the context of responsible parenthood, rather than as a means of liberating women. Such titles as planned parenthood and family planning were adopted by the promoters of birth control advisedly, both to give the subject its broader dimensions and to win more adherents for the movement.

The world-wide recognition of this question has led the United Nations Commission on the Status of Women (after some hesitation)

49

finally to move and study the whole question of family planning and its relationship to the Status of Women, especially in the overpopulated parts of the world. The Commission appointed one of its members a special rapporteur, whose task is to produce a full report on this subject, based on surveys as well as case studies from various countries.

The present interest of nations in family planning obviously did not come from a concern over women's status and well-being. It came mainly from the fact that the pressure of growing population began to hamper their national development. Family planning programmes began to be established in many of the overpopulated nations as a means of controlling population growth, but certainly not in recognition of women's rights.

Fertility control however meant voluntary decision on the part of families, especially women, to control family size. Where women are uneducated, where the woman's role is mainly restricted to the family, and where she is dependent and lacking in ambition, it is unlikely that the concept of family planning will find ready acceptance. In most developing countries of the world women are poor and illiterate for the most part. Some governments therefore are beginning to take a new look at the status of women in their countries and to see in their emancipation and advancement perhaps a solution to this gigantic problem. This is true of at least India, Pakistan, Tunisia, and Jamaica, where official statements to this effect have been reproduced in UN documents.

Let me now take Egypt as an example of an overpopulated developing country and see how the role of women is related to the problem of population growth and control and to the possible success of the family planning programme.

Egypt is a typically developing country whose efforts to modernize and develop are offset by its accelerating population growth. The average per capita share of the cropped area was reduced from 0.71 acres in 1879 to 0.39 in 1960. It is a predominantly agricultural country with very little natural resources. Its mortality rate began to decline after the Second World War before economic planning had taken place, and it further declined after the 1952 Revolution due to the expansion of free medical care. The mortality rate declined between 1906 and 1966 from 27 per 1,000 to 15 per 1,000 which is still considered high. Its birth rate is 42 per 1,000 and its growth rate is 2.7 percent. The present population of Egypt is 30 million and it is expected to double in 26 years.

A family planning programme was launched in Egypt in 1966, again not in recognition of women's rights but mainly to cope with the accelerating population growth. In the implementation of the programme, however, the status of women began to assert itself as one of the important elements to be reckoned with.

50

Let me first take up the traditional role of women which affects their attitude to childbearing. The one-sided domestic role of women in Egypt had been expressed for long centuries in the form of female segregation called Harem. Women of the upper class led a life of idleness and frustration within closed walls, and they set the pattern for the rest of the female population — even though the poorer women could not afford the luxury of such seclusion. Education was considered a waste of time and a danger to femininity. Work for women was considered both harmful and degrading as it implied the incapacity of the head of the family to provide for his womenfolks. Moreover work gave women the opportunity to mix with the other sex, and women's morality was thought to be safeguarded only by strict seclusion. Obviously childbearing became the raison d'etre of the Harem lady.

The insecure position of the woman in the family is also regarded as an important factor in her attitude to childbearing. Under the present family law the husband has privileges and responsibilities not shared by his wife that are reminiscent of the social values of patriarchal extended family systems. A man still has the right to marry more than one wife and to divorce his wife at will without recourse to court. The Moslem women, on the other hand, once married (by her freely signed consent) cannot obtain divorce except through a court ruling on the basis of certain specified grounds.

Clipping a husband's wings by burdening him with any number of children is still the standard traditional manoeuver of wives to keep their husbands from marrying another woman. And this argument has been used many times in the effort to amend family laws which have not yet been amended. In a predominantly agrarian society where marriage is an economic necessity and children an economic asset and a future security for their parents in old age, children are wanted in large numbers to compensate for the high child mortality which started to decline only recently and, hence, a large measure of the status of the woman is derived from her childbearing potential.

In traditional Egyptian society marriage has the additional value from a moral point of view in protecting a girl's chastity. The highest premium indeed is placed on a girl's virginity. Hence the tradition of early marriage. The legal minimum marriage age is 16 for girls and 18 for boys, but in some cases it has been proved that girls get married even below that legal age in contravention of the law. Statistics for the years 1940, 1950, and 1960 indicated that 75 percent of all marriages are contracted before the wife is 25. A study of three villages in Giza not far from Cairo revealed marriage to be contracted below the minimum age in contravention of the law.[3]

Statistically the value of marriage in Egypt is reflected in the fact that 98 percent of Egyptian women who had reached the end of their childbearing age had been married at one time or another.[1]

Family planning was not an issue in the movement for the emancipation of the Egyptian woman which started in Egypt in the early part of the twentieth century. Taboos of all kinds surrounded the question of birth control, even though, from the religious point of view, it was known to religious authorities at least that the prophet Mohammad had permitted the practice under certain conditions. Nevertheless the successful efforts of the Egyptian feminists were bound to be of major assistance to the family planning programme, a fact which is just being recognized.

The veil was the first target of the feminist movement as the symbol of female segregation. Mrs. Hoda Sharawi, the founder of the movement removed it in public in a dramatic gesture of public protest. The arguments of the early feminists were based, on the one hand, on consideration of women's human rights, and, on the other, on the liberal interpretation of the Moslem religion. Islam has long given women independent legal and property rights that still have not been acquired by women in some European societies. Mr. Kasim Amin blamed the ills and backwardness suffered by Egyptian society as a whole on the fact that Egyptian women had been prevented from playing their role as citizens in the life of the community. Sheikh Mohammad Abdou, an eminent Moslem scholar, campaigned for the amendment of marriage laws in conformity with what he regarded as the truly progressive spirit of Islam.

The feminist movement succeeded in gaining for women the right of education. Education was bound to develop in women a new concept of self that would reject the traditionally prescribed roles and become an important factor in the acceptance of such new values as family planning.

Until 1922 there was only one secondary school for girls, with a handful of students. Gradually educational opportunities for women were expanded until education through the university became free and accessible to men and women on equal terms. As a result women began to move into educational and employment spheres which had been for a long time the preserves of men. Our four or five universities are now attended by at least 30,000 women, to whom all studies are accessible without discrimination; as a result we already have thousands of women working in engineering, aeronautics, agriculture, animal husbandry, nuclear physics, medicine, etc.

Education, by preparing women for respectable professional employment, served to remove gradually the traditional stigma attached to work for women in general. Women's employment is another major factor which is likely to influence fertility patterns. More recently in 1966 the right of

52

women to work was proclaimed by the National Charter as equivalent to life itself, and described "as a practical affirmation of human existence, a principle which applies equally to men and women."

In spite of tradition and thanks to education and later to the enforcement of socialist measures the image of the ideal woman was dramatically transformed, from the veil and seclusion to co-education and gainful employment side by side with men. Barriers began to break down between men and women, between masculine and feminine jobs.

Educated women, especially when they are gainfully employed, have come to feel less insecure over their husband's rights to divorce or marry more than one wife. More divorce cases are, in fact, initiated by educated women against their husbands, and the problem, as I have seen it, is how to deprive the husband from his right *not* to divorce his wife, as she cannot get rid of him except through court ruling. As to polygamy, it could be said to be non-existent among the educated groups (according to official statistics it occurs only in three percent of all marriages).

However these changes have not touched all women. In fact when we look at statistics and numbers we find that while the number of educated women is growing fast, the number of illiterates is apparently growing faster. An analysis of the 1960 Census revealed that 89 percent of the married female population is still illiterate.[1] Seventy-four percent of women of university education have gainful employment.

The emancipation and advancement of women is certainly not an easy process, since it is directly connected with the general state of development of a country – a process which in turn is likely to be undermined by excessive population growth.

In the implementation of the family planning programme the vulnerability of the poor illiterate woman is indeed a major obstacle; and the independence of the educated woman is its hope for success. For example, the relation of women's education to fertility, as taken from the 1960 Census, is as follows: Illiterate mothers had an average of 4.05 children per married woman, those with primary education had 3.66, and those with secondary and university education had 1.86 children. The difference was even more significant when a comparative study was made of these groups after a marriage duration of 30 to 35 years. The illiterate mothers had an average of 7.11 children, those with primary education 6.06, and those with secondary and university education 3.08 children.[2]

A study of the clinic records of voluntary associations revealed a negative correlation between the size of the family and the standard of education that was more conspicuous in relation to the wife's education than to that of her husband. These clinics, however, because they offer free services, were attended mostly by poorer uneducated women, the majority of whom had come after they had already contributed their share to the population explosion. Only a few of them had begun to appreciate small family size or the value of spacing. The vast majority of the cases had admitted having resorted to illegally induced abortions at least once. One of the women admitted to having had 11 abortions.

If the sample studied in our clinics is truly representative of the records in the larger programmes, then there is no doubt but that the family planning programme so far is contributing enormously to the health and well-being of many women who may have otherwise undergone illegal and dangerous abortions. However, its contribution to fertility control is still limited.

What the programme has also achieved is acceptance by the people of birth control as a legitimate practice for the family. In Egypt, there is more talk than ever before of the importance of family limitation to the welfare of the individuals, of the families, and of the nation. Although there is understandably still a wide gap between theory and practice, there is still hope that social change in terms of new family-size values need not wait for basic socio-economic development, for a start could be made by appealing to women's basic needs as mothers. This is attempted in my country by the integration of the Egyptian family planning programme with maternal and child health services on the one hand, and with other child care services, namely nursery schools, on the other. These channels give the mother greater reassurance as to the survival of her children, and help develop in her higher levels of aspirations for them and a new sense of the value of each individual child.

Another hopeful trend which is expected to accelerate social change is the recognition and encouragement of the role of women volunteers in the family planning programme. Feminine leadership has asserted itself as an important element in the successful implementation of this programme, not only in the main cities but also in some provincial towns and villages. Recently established leadership training programmes for women include family planning as a high priority item.

There are, according to some eminent sociologists, other means of inducing an early change of attitude towards family size, mainly in the line of governmental legislation policies. Legislative action to discourage large families is recommended in such areas as family law, social benefits, taxation, labour laws, etc., and some of these have a direct bearing on the status of women. However these ideas have not yet gained recognition in Egypt.

In conclusion, as already noted, the relationship between the status of women and family planning did not come to attention until recently. The two movements, emancipation of women and family planning, started and grew separately, but many people are beginning to see them moving closer together, especially in developing countries where the relationship between the role of women and the successful implementation of family planning programmes is being established more and more frequently.

1. — Anne-Marie Dourben-Rollier. *La Verite sur l'Abortement.*
2. — *Family Planning and the Status of Women*, UN Interim Report to the Commission on the Status of Woman in the UN.
3. — Haifa Shanawani. *Factors influencing fertility in the UAR.*

CATHOLICS AND BIRTH CONTROL AFTER "HUMANAE VITAE"

Louis Dupré

Louis Dupré, born in Belgium, received his training in theology at Louvain being granted both the Ph.D. and Licentiate in Theology with high honours. He joined the faculty of Georgetown University in Washington, D.C. and rapidly gained an international reputation.

Professor Dupré has published widely in philosophical and theological journals on topics such as faith, morality, ecumenism, Marxism, and birth control. His books include "Contraception and Catholics", 1964, and "The Philosophical Foundations of Marxism", 1966.

In Washington he has taken a liberal position in the discussion of birth control and has been in constant dialogue with more conservative elements of the Roman Catholic Church. He has urged that government establish liberal policies on family planning in testimony before U.S. Congressional Committees.

In our western world today the Catholic Church, to which I belong, is the one major body that officially opposes artificial birth control, and in the Church the decisive factor of opposition has been Pope Paul's recent Encyclical *Humanae Vitae*. You will therefore not consider it out of place, I hope, if I address myself to the problems created by this Encyclical and if I try to define where precisely we stand today. To make my statement more than one man's opinion I shall deliberately abstain from any criticism of the content of the Encyclical. I also, in order to speak for the majority of my fellow Catholics, shall take a rather conservative position, but neither one of these positions, abstaining from criticism and taking a conservative theological position, is indispensable to Catholics. I also hope that the non-Catholics will bear with me patiently when I go through somewhat tedious details necessary for an understanding of the argument.

What kind of assent does *Humanae Vitae* require? In paragraph 28 of his Encyclical Pope Paul himself asks for a "loyal internal and external obedience to the teaching authority of the Church." A footnote at that point refers to Vatican II's Constitution on the Church which states that allegiance of the will and the intellect should be given in an entirely special way to the authentic teaching authority of the Roman pontiff even when he is not speaking *ex cathedra*. This is obviously more than mere external conformity. Yet the Constitution of the Vatican Council does not explain of what precisely the "internal assent" to such documents consists. It refers instead to the accepted manuals of theology. Now these manuals describe the assent as both *religious*, that is, founded upon the teaching authority of the Church and not merely upon the intrinsic merit of the arguments (in other words the arguments may be pretty bad but you still give an assent because of the authority of the Church), and secondly the assent is described as being *conditional*, that is, not absolute as in the case of what we Catholics call the infallible teaching authority of the Church. My apologies for all these distinctions. The main point here is that the Encyclical refers to the Vatican Council, that the Vatican Council refers to the accepted, and I may add, traditional manuals of theology, and these manuals themselves state that the assent should be conditional. The conditions for withholding assent are differently defined in different manuals. One famous textbook of the beginning of the century, a very traditional one that is no longer used, states very clearly: "Assent is prudently suspended when there first appear sufficient motives for doubting."[1] Another from 1891 holds that religious assent is owed when nothing could prudently persuade one to suspend it.[2] One textbook even mentions, as one of the ways to prevent error in the Church from spreading by means of the Pope's teaching authority, the faithful's withholding of internal assent.[3]

The conclusion follows that the believer should give his assent only when he can do so without violating his intellectual integrity. This interpretation is confirmed by most hierarchies in the western world, more particularly by the directives of the Belgian bishops in their Pastoral Letter on the Encyclical when they say, and in saying this they merely restate the traditional doctrine: "Someone, however, who is competent in the matter under consideration and capable of forming a personal and well-founded judgment—which necessarily presupposes a sufficient amount of know-ledge—may after a serious examination before God come to other conclusions on certain points. In such as case he has the right to follow his conviction provided that he remains sincerely disposed to continue his inquiry."[4]

I would say that common sense would lead to the same conclusion. If a document is not infallible, not even in the eyes of those who wrote it, then it is intellectually not justifiable to give an absolute assent where one knows the possibility of error exists. It has a built-in possibility by being an ordinary document. Let me ask you the question. Where would theology be today if theologians had not positively recognized the fact that a non-infallible declaration could be false or inadequate? We would be stuck with some strange things indeed in the Catholic Church. Is it not

58

possible, however, to consider the Encyclical as the final word in a long uninterrupted teaching tradition which would make it virtually infallible or, as some theologians have said, "definable"? Again apologies for the esoteric distinctions. Well, my answer to that is that neither the Pope nor the Council did define formally the content of the Encyclical, and that even at the time of *Casti Connubii*, the previous Encyclical of Pope Pius XI, which stated this doctrine, and which was more or less generally accepted, there were enough theologians who doubted whether the Church's position on this problem could claim the authority of a permanent tradition. This is a new problem. So let us not speak about the permanent tradition. Even fewer are found today to defend the existence of a unanimous tradition now that historical studies have made it obvious that no simple conclusions can be drawn from so complex a past as the moral tradition of the Catholic Church. If anything, the Church is today more and more divided on this issue.

Now these remarks are not intended to downgrade the importance of the papal pronouncement for Catholics. But I discern in some circles, and coming from Washington I am in a particularly good position to discern this, a tendency to promote the Encyclical into an infallible document commanding absolute assent. Karl Rahner, like most other Catholic theologians, firmly disagrees with this interpretation: "At no point in the Encyclical do we perceive the formulation which can arouse the impression that it is a matter of a formal definition. We may even say that the formulations in this respect are couched more prudently than perhaps the declarations of Pius XI on the same question."[5]

Aside from the objective status of the Encyclical, the authority, there still is the much more fundamental question concerning what ought to be the ultimate norm of morality for all men, Christians and non-Christians alike, namely their conscience. Non-Catholics may think that conscience is the norm of morality for other Christians but not for Catholics. This opinion, as I hope to show, is false. Respect for the individual conscience was clearly implied in the Vatican Council's Declaration on Religious Freedom. Nor is this a new insight—even though I admit official doctrine in the past can hardly be said to have heeded it—because moral theology has for centuries recognized that man must follow his conscience even if it is wrong. John Henry Newman as a Catholic expressed this attitude of respect for conscience most forcefully in his famous letter to the Duke of Norfolk: "Certainly if I am obliged to bring religion into after dinner toasts. . . . I shall drink, to the Pope, if you please, . . . still, to conscience first, and to the Pope afterwards." This doctrine was applied directly to the Encyclical by the pastoral letter of the hierarchy of England and Wales: "Neither this encyclical nor any other document of Church takes away from us our right and duty to follow our conscience. The Pope, bishop, clergy and faithful must all be true to conscience." In agreement with this position but perhaps even more forceful was the Declaration of your own Canadian hierarchy: "In accord with the accepted principles of moral theology, if these persons who experience a conflict of duties in attempting to observe the teaching of the encyclical have tried sincerely, but without success, to pursue a line of conduct in keeping with the given directives, they may be safely assured that whoever honestly chooses that course which seems right to him, does so in good conscience."

That conscience is the ultimate norm of morality does not imply that the Church has no teaching authority in moral matters and that each Catholic decides exclusively according to his own private insights. There has been an attempt by some ecclesiastics—most particularly by Cardinal O'Boyle in Washington—to reduce any form of dissent to an outright dismissal of objective Church doctrine or even to reduce it to a dismissal of all objective moral norms. As if anybody who did not fully agree with this document did not accept an objective morality. This interpretation I strongly oppose. The words that are constantly used by these people are "situation ethics" and "new morality." I venture to say that there is quite a space between a purely subjectivist situation ethics which accepts no objective principles and the rigid objectivism which considers itself bound by the external norms of the Church even when these norms conflict with what the individual conscience judges to be ultimately acceptable. There is quite a space in between these two. Vatican II gave a more nuanced interpretation of the moral teaching of the Church: "In the formation of their consciences the Christian faithful ought *carefully to attend to* the sacred and certain doctrine of the Church." This text says precisely what should be said about all extrinsic moral norms, that is, norms imposed from without: they ought to be considered carefully, but they do not replace individual moral judgment because nothing replaces conscience.

Any extrinsically provided rule, no matter how sacred, must still be *recognized* by the individual as *objectively* true, as acceptable. Otherwise he runs the risk of accepting as objective rules what may in fact not be more than someone else's subjective convictions. So it is in the name of moral objectivity or of objective morality that I defend the right of conscience. Without a conscience that accepts a rule as objective the rule is not objective, it becomes arbitrary. This risk of taking merely someone else's opinions is always present as long as the possibility of error exists, and that possibility does exist in the non-infallible teaching of the Church such as the present Encyclical. It is a very important point in morality, that an extrinsic rule, a rule imposed from without, can become an objective norm for action in the individual only *when it is perceived as such*, when someone sees that it is that way, that it ought to be that way. Objectivity cannot exist without a subject to accept and to perceive it as objective. A moral act to be moral must always contain a subjective acceptance which converts an external rule into a valid principle of action. To overlook this subjective element does not make you more objectively moral, but it destroys the morality of the act altogether. So don't try to out-objectivize objectivity by saying I don't want to look into the matter I accept it blindly. By doing that, by accepting something as objectively true which you find subjectively false you act against your conscience and, if you are an informed person at least, you act against your conscience and you destroy morality. Following this rather obvious line of thought one cannot but conclude that a Christian may responsibly decide in accordance with his conscience to follow another line of action than the one prescribed in the Encyclical, if, as the Belgian bishops and as traditional theology state, he is competent in the matter.

Finally, and here I come to my third point, what the individual Catholic will do in his own life remains ultimately a matter of informed conscience, to be decided by each one for himself in the light of the Church's teaching. Yet even if he does unconditionally accept the guidelines of the Encyclical, and this for the time being I will accept to be the case here, even then he will still be faced with the problems of overpopulation in underdeveloped areas abroad and at home. Although this problem involves mostly non-Catholics it nevertheless requires a decision on his part, because the government which he elects and to which he pays taxes is very much involved in the solution of these problems. I understand that there is a good chance that very soon here in Canada also contraception will no longer be illegal, not even nominally illegal. Must a Catholic then abstain from participation in public programmes, government sponsored programmes, foreign aid programmes, that promote artificial birth control? That is the question. Or must he perhaps positively attempt to obstruct such programmes? I would say that Catholics as well as all other people have a positive responsibility in the present population crisis, and they cannot just sit back and wait until the non-Catholics solve the problem, although this is what they have usually done in the past. In taking up this responsibility the Catholic can hardly expect everyone to adopt the official views of his Church.

Yet I would say the moral problem involved in the support of government sponsored programmes of birth control is not whether one is personally convinced of the morality of the various methods of contraception, but whether one is willing to allow others to make available the means which they, by an informed choice, can adopt or reject according to their own conscience, and not according to your Catholic conscience. That is the problem. The positive obligation to respect the religious and moral convictions of those who do not share their faith holds eminently true for Catholics, who were recently reminded in the Vatican Council: "No one is to be forced to act in a manner contrary to his own beliefs *nor is anyone to be restrained from acting in accordance with his own beliefs*, whether privately or publicly, whether alone or in association with others, within due limits." It would seem, though, that Catholics who, because of personal moral views, or because of the moral views of their Church, prevent legislation which would allow people to cope with a most urgent economic problem according to the dictates of these people's own consciences, that such Catholics are paying only lip service to the Council's directives. Religious freedom demands more than non-interference with someone else's non-existent freedom. It includes giving and giving positively a choice to those who had no choice and even making accessible information of which the others might not even have suspected the existence. The information we are offering by giving information on birth control is not a new way of violating the moral law; it is an efficient means to attain an end which is universally recognized as a moral good. The end is good, the Church agrees with that. The means itself is considered moral by the great majority of those who are acquainted with it, by the great majority of non-Catholics; it is considered doubtful or even immoral by members of one major group, to which I belong. But why should this personal dissent of a relatively small minority in the world be a reason for depriving the poor and the underprivileged of the right of practising their freedom according to their conscience rather than to mine?

Finally, one last word on an intricate problem: is the distribution of birth control information the task of governments? The problem may sound somewhat academic at the present in Canada. It soon may become a practical problem. To what extent does the common good require government intervention into the private life of its citizens? That is the question. I think the moral answer to this question is: Only to the extent that the common good urgently demands such intervention, and even then with the greatest possible precautions for safeguarding the freedom of the individual. This is particularly the case of course when the government of one state assists citizens of another state, as in a foreign aid programme. Yet two points are to be made in this respect. First, the absolute separation between one state and another, which is characteristic of the so-called "modern" period of history, no longer exists today. We are all in the same boat. Whether we like it or not, we are inseparably united in the adventure of contemporary life, and foreign aid is only a practical recognition of a *de facto* existing situation of togetherness. Second, the need is *most* urgent in some of the poorest countries and in some of the poorest areas of our own countries. In fact, it is so urgent that its urgency surpasses that of any nutritional aid, for a continuation of the present growth rate will soon defeat the possibilities of even the most extensive food programme. As I heard the Secretary of Agriculture of the United States of America say one time, there just is not enough to go around at a certain point, no matter what we do. If, then, we have the right and the obligation to assist foreign nations in their immediate needs, we definitely are allowed to help them in their immediate needs, and we definitely are allowed to help them in preventing an emergency for which there will soon no longer be an immediate solution available. You know that once it is too late in this business, it is too late. You cannot unmake people. I venture to say that some countries may already have reached such an emergency.

Here, again, it is in the name of respect for people's freedom, the freedom to survive rather than to sink even deeper into abjection, that Catholics ought to cooperate actively in making birth control available to their neighbours in need at home and abroad.

1. – C. Pesch, *Praelectiones Dogmaticae* (1915), Vol. I, p. 370.

2. – Palmieri, *De Romano Pontifice*, p. 7199.

3. – Lercher, *Institutiones Theologiae Dogmaticae* (1924-34), Vol. I, p. 297. My information on this and the other manuals is derived from an unpublished paper by Harry McSorley.

4. – English Translation, *National Catholic Reporter*, Sept. 11, 1968, p. 7.

5. – "On the Encyclical *Humanae Vitae*," *Stimmen der Zeit*, September 1968. (English Translation, *National Catholic Reporter*, September 18, 1968, p. 6.)

IMPACT OF FAMILY PLANNING IN CANADA

June Callwood

June Callwood, born in Chatham, Ontario in 1924, is married to Toronto journalist Trent Frayne. They have four children.

Miss Callwood's first newspaper work was in Brantford and then later at the Toronto Globe and Mail. Following her marriage in 1944 she began publishing in magazines often on topics related to family life, status of women and civil liberties and is still a prolific writer. She appears frequently on Canadian radio and television programmes.

Miss Callwood has been active in organizations such as the Canadian Civil Liberties Association, Citizen's Housing Committee, Canadian Mental Health Association. Her activities as landlady of Digger House in Toronto, dedicated to provide a temporary home for itinerant youth, has sometimes aroused the suspicions of Toronto's Establishment and constabulary.

This Teach-In is concerned with the world population crisis, which in most parts of the globe is related to numbers. It may therefore seem incongruous that it is being held in Canada, an empty land particularly when seen from the air, a country of only 20 million people strung out along its southern border, a nation with a rapidly dropping birthrate, and one of those affluent, elite nations with a massive statistical advantage in television sets, and indoor plumbing and life insurance, a country removed by abstraction and distraction from the world population explosion on its doorstep. It is, after all, happening at least one ocean away and it is happening almost exclusively to people who are not white; Canadians are not heartless, but it is difficult for our imaginations to encompass the possibility that a black, yellow or brown person can feel pain as exquisitely as we do,—or hunger, or hope.

Despite the blinker effect of our whiteness, the central issues of the population explosion—which are birth control and concern for life—are as valid in Canada as they are in India or Egypt or Peru or anywhere. This is a country which can feed ,its population—only slightly less than one-quarter of Canadians are destitute, according to the recent report of the Economic Council of Canada, and this proportion is, by world standards, a stunning achievement. This is a country which can educate its population—not yet in a manner which produces enthusiasm for learning or a young person equipped to understand himself and his society, but nevertheless almost all our children are in school past the elementary level.

And this is a country which can almost house its population. For much of the population, it does not do so in a manner which is conducive to health or sanity, but there are no families wandering the highways with their belongings on their backs. In fact we take housekeeping care to to keep them off the streets, by one means or another. In a pinch, there is always the vagrancy law—in Canada it is a criminal offence to be poor and homeless and there is a cell in a stone building awaiting the offender.

The glaring problems of the underdeveloped countries are not here. Instead we bear in full measure the burdens of the developed countries: adults so hassled that their life-loving instincts are pounded flat; prisons and mental hospitals bursting with the lonely, the sick and the angry; a generation of teenagers who commit the partial suicide of alcohol, drugs, promiscuous sex and violence as a technique for enduring their existence. On this continent total suicide is the second most frequent cause of death in teenagers, with motor vehicle accidents first, and no way of gauging what portion of motor vehicle accidents are the result of collapsed self-esteem and wish for death. We have small children in this country being brutalized to insanity, perversion, or death by parents who are deranged, or who are desperate with financial or marital problems or drink, or who are mentally retarded and cannot believe that bedwetting will not be cured by burning a child's palms with matches. There are so many children in homes which are destroying them that no Children's Aid Society in Canada has a sufficient budget to come to the aid of all *that they know about.* Some time ago the Children's Aid Society in Middlesex County, a not particularly congested or deprived part of Ontario, estimated that if all the children who needed help in that district could receive it, five hundred would be removed from their homes at once.

And, finally, this affluent and emerged country is almost unique in the world in its indifference to the fate of its most powerless citizens, its babies. A child in the Phillipines may be ill-fed and ill-educated, but he is not ill-loved; a little boy in Africa is naked for want of clothes, but he is not neglected; a child in Spain wanders around the town, an object of fond regard and attentiveness; in North American Indian tribes, a little person is the property and responsibility of every member of the tribe—a mother's inability to care for him does not leave the child bereft.

We in Canada know from books that human love and trust are skills taught non-verbally in a very simple, very beautiful way: by giving an infant consistent affectionate care from one person throughout the most crucial part of his life, the first fifteen months. We know that a baby, out of the buzzing confusion of his frightening environment, has to make sense about his own being from the only clues at hand, the adults who care for him. He cannot do otherwise but hate and reject if he is hated and rejected; he cannot be other than baffled and anxious if the faces keep changing before he can figure them out; he cannot miss feeling confident, and jubilant, and valuable, if his mother loves him and can stay nearby. That priceless gift is abundant in backward countries; this nation, one of the few on earth where the classic experiments with maternal deprivation are widely known, is also one of the few on earth which deprives babies of maternal love on a wide scale. Civilization's most sophisticated advance, it appears, is this—that wretched and wrecked adults are free to wreck babies.

We permit anyone to raise a baby, we permit sadists, baby-haters, infantile people, and people who are hysterically frightened. The criterion is fertility. We do not ask about desire for parenthood, or preparation for parenthood, or competence, sanity, or that there is a home free from roaches and rats, or a level of income that can reduce that terrible strain that poverty imposes on gentleness and compassion and humour. These do not matter. In this country the definition of mother is a functioning uterus.

In fact, we impel motherhood upon females. The only legal alternative to motherhood at the present time is celibacy. It's a state which may seem admirable to many, and sad to many others, but is not in either case nature's biological plan for our species. The stance of the law is very peculiar: it suggests that sex is wrong-doing, hence having a baby is the punishment that fits the crime. The punishment, after a brief interval, falls entirely on the baby, who is routed straight through the normal life span with a ticket that reads INVALID, unless it is his great luck to have from his first breath a good adoptive home or a mother who changed her mind. It is not unfair to say that this is comparatively unusual, since it is possible that more than half of all pregnancies are unwanted; evidence of this is found in those countries which permit unlimited abortion on demand, where abortions promptly exceeded the birthrate.

When a woman expresses unwillingness to have a baby there is something wrong. It may be sociological, physiological, psychological, economic, or a combination of them, which is more common. We speak today of having a just society, where the quality of life is of some concern: but let us demonstrate it by allowing the quality of the baby's life to enter into the decision. If housing is the factor which accounts for the woman's unwillingness to have a baby, shouldn't we care enough about that baby to provide a proper shelter for him? If it is economic, can we not afford to subsidize that baby—and not so meanly, that the baby and the mother live a life of desperation? If the woman is working, and must work either to fulfill her own needs or to support the family, or both together, can society not offer her some alternatives, such as maternity leave, or part-time employment, or subsidization, and day-care for the baby, that is superb day-care for the baby? And there are women who are just apprehensive, and they can be easily reassured; and all women should be informed that there is a possible guilt reaction which may be crippling if there has been an abortion; if the women entertains the thought, however fleetingly, that she is not aborting a foetus but that she is murdering a baby, the repercussions to her mental stability, her self-esteem, may be devastating.

But, finally, when all the offers of help and counselling have been made, society is lacking in integrity if it does not step aside and permit the woman to make a free choice on her own, whether to make an appointment with her doctor for a D and C or to accept one of the alternatives.

Many say that unlimited distribution of birth control devices and permitting legal abortions on demand would tear the fabric of our society, would destroy decency and goodness. I submit that the fabric of our society is in rags, and decency and goodness are having a very bad time. We are stacking young families now in apartment houses, where the women go mad, the men desert, the small children become desperate and the older ones furious. In one area of Metropolitan Toronto, where there is a good deal of Ontario Housing Corporation highrise, there has been a 76 percent increase in delinquency, a 50 percent increase in illegitimate births, a 400 percent increase in children seen by the Children's Aid Society; in one school in that area, with 800 students, 200 are in urgent need of psychiatric services. Very few of them will get it. Very few of the babies born under the choking frustrating conditions in multiple housing units cannot be described as "high risk" babies, psychologically so mutilated that they are the living dead.

It is tempting to imagine a society in which every baby was wanted—not just every baby born to articulate middle-class people, who already have sufficient control over their own procreation so that this is within reach, but every baby born anywhere. What a gift, what a start, to have a mother who is glad to see you. It would offer no guarantee of lifelong happiness, it could not prevent the big disasters of death, illness, deformity, or the ones which splatter every lifetime, the discouragements, injustices and betrayals. But the baby could go forth into whatever fate decides, armed against total collapse with the one weapon that matters, the hallelujah chorus of feeling safe in the human race.

Consider the impact on this country if every baby was welcomed at birth. It would be felt first in the schools, which are fully aware at last that ability to learn is related to emotional harmony, and that frightened, angry, despairing children cannot learn at all. It would show itself eight or nine years after it had begun in juvenile crime statistics, which are composed largely of children reacting to more stress than they can bear. The training schools would begin to empty, and the group homes where disturbed children are trying to respond to the first loving concern many of them have ever experienced, and then the jails and mental hospitals would become less populated. And everywhere on the streets it would be seen that people who feel good about themselves feel good about strangers, and hostility and loneliness would lift a little, maybe even to such a degree that they would be bearable.

It would not be perfect, of course. There is more to emotional disturbance and the impulse to murder than lack of mother love—there are the mystery factors in the chromosomes and simple bad luck and perversity. The world would still be in a sufficient amount of mess to give cheerful employment to the litter-bearers, the psychologists, social workers and psychiatrists. But it would be improved, it would be dazzling.

I don't think there is any longer time or money enough to continue the near futile repair of lives damaged by early lack of affection. We do not have enough group homes to fill the need, and it isn't feasible that we can get enough, not only because of lack of funds but also because such homes require a lot of staff, and all must have compassionate hearts and a degree of emotional balance. These are in short supply for the same reason that the group homes are needed: mass, unselected motherhood inflicted too often on women who are not mothers.

We are living in a time of fearful change, under panic conditions; it is as though the air raid siren has been wailing for the past ten years and our nerves are wrecked with the suspense of waiting for the planes. We are very hard on ourselves: we are drinking too much, drugging ourselves too much, being angry and scared too much, venting ourselves on our joyless children too much, and hating what we can't understand all too readily. This country doesn't have an explosion population problem, but it has a misery population problem of urgent magnitude.

We can make a simple start to unravel the mess: we can guarantee that every baby born will receive loving care. There are concomitants, of course: an environment in which loving care is feasible involves housing that is adjusted to human needs for recreation, privacy, contact with earth, and an income that permits breathing room. Protection of the young, as an official policy, would mean support and sympathy for mothers and also recognition of the often minimized role of fathers, who are the crucial element in every family. Paternal damage, through absenteeism, indifference or hostility, is a growing factor in the case histories of what is happening to our teenagers, the most discouraged ones—males in our society are under savage pressure to find dignity and confidence for themselves: there is no risk or adventure any more against which men can measure themselves and come to believe in their virility and courage. Concern that a baby reach his potential without gross violation would have to encompass the needs of a man to feel triumphantly male, if his son and daughter are to feel triumphant about their gender.

In short, let us regard our human resources as our first priority, and shape our laws and institutions to fit what we know of human development and needs. Science has provided us with safe birth control techniques. If it is not too late, it is the greatest boon available to man. When all babies have a good life, the world will be a very safe place indeed.

THE IMPERIALISM OF POPULATION CONTROL

Brewster Kneen

Brewster Kneen was born in Cleveland in 1933. He married Cathleen Rosenberg in 1964; they have two children. They came to Toronto in 1965 and became involved in a number of social action programs almost immediately.

Mr. Kneen studied economics at Cornell, spent two years in the U.S. Navy, then continued his education at Edinburgh University, Union Theological Seminary, and the London School of Economics.

Though he studied theology, Mr. Kneen was not ordained. He did student work for the Fellowship of Reconciliation throughout the U.S.A. from 1961 to 1964. In Canada he became deeply involved in the development of the New Left student movement and was also the National Secretary of the Canadian Fellowship of Reconciliation.

His travels since 1958 include extensive periods in Eastern and Western Europe. He is a member of the Continuation Committee of the Christian Peace Conference. He is a full-time resource person with the Centre for the Study of Institutions and Theology at Rochdale College.

Mr. Kneen is well known as a broadcaster and commentator on public affairs radio programs, as well as a speaker and seminar leader. He has published papers titled "Revolution and Intervention" in 1966, "Concerning Marxist-Christian Dialogue" in 1966, and "The New Consciousness" in 1967.

Is population size—the crisis of numbers—really a value-free technical matter? Or is it a socio-political matter involving a great many variables, some known and some unknown, that pose questions about the style and quality of human life that mankind has not yet really taken seriously in any large scale way, except for China?

I do not want to discuss the legitimacy of birth control *per se*. In fact, I think that birth control information and equipment ought to be available to everyone, men and women, regardless of age or status, without cost or restriction. It ought' to be available in the same way as chest x-rays are now, and paid for out of public funds. If the profit were taken out of the production and distribution of birth control equipment, by the way, it would be interesting to see what would happen to "public interest" and some of the more strident voices calling for population control and predicting dire consequences if we do not control population.

There are three orders of questions that must be discussed if we are openly and honestly to formulate or even discuss a policy of population control or simply the problem of population size: analytical questions, dealing with the purportedly factual material; questions concerning the decision-making process itself; and moral or value questions which must form the basis of the actual decision-making.

The Analytical Questions

What can we say about population growth and trends, about natural resources and food, about human consumption and its forms? Is it a fact that there will be severe famines in 1975 or is this prophecy based on certain rather questionable statistics? What do we know about China and is China accounted for in the statistics we use? If we have not included China in all of our calculations—China with its quarter of the world's population—what significance can any of our extrapolations or predictions have? What, for that matter, do we really know about population trends in the U.S. or Canada that could give us a reasonable basis for prediction? Will the present student generation bear children in the same pattern as those of us five or ten years older? Will the social upheaval that is taking shape in the U.S. be without significance for family size and structure? Or if population growth is the biggest obstacle to our concept of economic growth or development, how does one account for the apparent fact that two Latin American countries with very high birth rates, Mexico and Venezuela, also have high rates of economic growth, or, on the contrary, that countries with relatively low rates of population growth, Argentina and Uruguay, also have low rates of economic growth? Obviously we do not know the validity of our statistics because we do not know or understand the functions of all the variables, such as the effects of secularization, the loss of the authority of the church, or the development of internal strife in a technological society, or the prolonged threat of nuclear war, or disaffection with a bourgeois life style. Even if we had sufficient and reliable statistics, how valid would extrapolation on the basis of these be since we cannot be sure what is liable to happen to human motivation and consciousness in unforeseen situations? What, for example, would be the psychological consequence for North Americans if we were to experience rapid population growth and achieve a density of population similar to that of Tokyo where 32 million people live in an area about the size of Metro Toronto?

I am simply suggesting that man is not an easily definable or statistically reliable phenomenon. I am suggesting that even at the level of

72

analytical method we must identify the operative concept of the nature of man. If man is a predetermined, unchanging animal without will or consciousness, then statistical extrapolation would be quite feasible, but one has first to accept a very particular view of man that is quite mechanistic, and this I do not accept.

Questions Concerning the Decision-making Process

If, in spite of what I have already said, we agree that the growth of population is a threat to mankind, how are we going to decide what to do about it and how are we going to implement our decision? Even in asking this question I have probably gone beyond the limits of many who would say that this is a problem for the experts. The fact is, we are all rather too well trained to leave all such difficult or complex or risky questions to some mystical body of experts, secure in the knowledge that this or that priestly cult of experts is more capable of deciding how I should live or when I should die than I am myself. But are there any experts on the subject of life and death or life style? Is the present incumbent in the White House really a person we wish to defer to on the issue of whether or not there is to be a nuclear war over Vietnam because the experts are leading America to defeat and disgrace? Or can a group of zoologists really be competent to tell the rest of us what life style is best or how many people can live together? Or are the police really competent to decide matters of morale and what length I should wear my hair? Who are the experts, and what makes them so? And how did we ever become convinced that we were not the very best experts concerning our own lives?

There are no experts in matters of life and death. We decide, for better or for worse, either by actively deciding or by deciding to default on the issues. I must make my own decision for life or death or forfeit my humanity. Only I have the right to decide what I shall die for. The technicians and experts have a responsibility to inform me of the possible consequence of my action and to suggest alternatives, and as a person the expert may try to convince me to change my behaviour, but as long as I am not imposing on his, there is nothing more he can or should do. But when my action, as in having many children when the expert is convinced that this is bad for all of us, imposes on others, then the matter is still not for the experts but for the public. Then the task of the expert is to inform the public and to persuade, but the decision must be made by the people as a whole. We have seen the tragic and inhuman consequences of decisions by the experts or authorities long enough.

For example, when "authorities" talk about the necessity of birth control and population limitation, I must ask myself who they are and who they speak for: the rich, the poor? Those concerned with the survival of special interest and certain benefits or those willing to see everything put at the disposal of the common good? I must ask what colour they are and what their class background is. I must ask if they are mature and liberated, or hung-up on personal identity or social status. More particularly, in this setting, I must ask, whether the people preaching birth control are in any way those with interests in the pharmaceutical business, or whether they are involved with industries that need more sophisticated markets and so need economic development of a certain sort and the production of consumers? Are they nations or political groups who have reasons to fear large numbers of people in other situations or are they people who must save the world for the American Way of Life?

Yet this sort of discussion still does not touch the question of the *mechanisms* of public decision-making, a virgin territory for us, and at this point there is little that can be said about mechanisms for making informed public decisions concerning goals, values and life style because we have simply neither developed nor experienced them, yet. All I can do here is urge that we give serious thought to the mechanisms and techniques of making significant decisions in a public way. The issue is being forced upon us, in fact, by the growing number of people who will no longer tolerate our traditional forms of manipulation and abuse.

If there are no experts to whom we can defer, then on what basis do we, common citizens, make decisions on such matters as population control? Hopefully we make them on the basis of values consciously held and applied. This leads us into the third category of questions.

Moral and Value Questions and the Implementation of Decisions

Alva Myrdal on the first page of her book *Nation and Family*, written in 1937, states well why we must raise these kinds of questions here. She says an established tendency to drive values underground, to make analysis appear scientific by omitting certain basic assumptions from the discussion, has too often emasculated the social sciences as agencies for rationality and social and political life. To be truly rational it is necessary to accept the obvious principle that a social programme, like a practical judgment, is a conclusion based upon premises of values as well as upon facts. And one of the most basic facts or values of the Western mentality, and I would say one of its most imperialist aspects, has been that of man's superiority over nature. This perversion of the biblical concept set forth in Genesis has produced a profoundly loveless attitude toward creation. And has reduced much of the world's natural resources to rubbish heaps, barren hills and cesspools. It has produced a presumptuous and arrogant belief that man can somehow escape the consequences of his own actions.

74

Conservationists, ecologists, and humanitarians in general have a major battle to wage to overcome the practices of centuries. And yet in doing this they tend to perpetuate the same imperialistic assumption, the same imperialistic attitude that man's ingenuity and will alone will save something for the future. And it seldom seems to occur to them that it might be better for all of us if we were to leave things and people alone for a while to see how they might do by themselves. This wreaks havoc of course with the traditional Christian concept of charity, because what does one do if the best thing we can do for others is to leave them alone? And even when the question of death control, the elimination of disease, and the prolongation of life, is suggested as a counter-measure, we must say that this is not an unmitigated good. This has been pointed out by Rainer Maria Rilke. Reproduction is now so enormous, and individual death is not so nicely carried out as it once was, but then that doesn't matter. It's quantity that counts. Who cares anything today for a finely finished death? No one. Even the rich who could after all afford the luxury of dying in full detail are beginning to be careless and indifferent. The wish to have a death of one's own is growing even rarer. A while yet and it will be just as rare as a life of one's own. And I wonder how many old people there are who have been kept alive when really they wish to relinquish their hold and to move on?

But what about the values on which our life proceeds? The values that are produced are wealth and our control over the world. Have we thoughtfully and consciously decided on how we are going to proceed, recognizing that we must accept responsibility for what we do even if we only obey order. For example, do we consider it the right of all people to choose their personal life style or do we through our diverse social institutions decree that it should be the prerogative of the affluent to choose a life style while the poor must take what we give them, including the degrading job, that we would ourselves refuse. Do we consider the possibility of a deliberately and thoughtfully chosen life style or do we again function primarily in terms of the class into which we were born? Or can we even speak about a meaningful personal life apart from consideration of the social good? Again, as China might suggest, this is contrary to our own experience.

These questions might seem far from the question of birth control and the crisis of numbers but again who is to decide the value of life and in what forms?

What about the claim that population control is essential to economic development, and economic development in turn essential to the welfare of people? Have we thought deeply and long about what we mean and imply by the phrase economic development? Since that more popular

Encyclical, the one on the development of peoples, economic development on our model has become as highly regarded as authority itself and largely by the same people. What about the other people? Is there any validity in our own model of development or even any good for other nations? What about the alternatives that have been experimented with in countries such as China or Cuba and to a lesser extent extent perhaps in some of the Eastern European countries? If we do no more than simply go on talking about economic development without considering what we mean and without thinking of its limitations and relative merits, then we can be justifiably accused of a kind of culture imperialism, because we will permit consideration of no alternatives to the model we proffer.

Obviously we have enormous economic power in this area. We speak for example of our concern with the economic development of the third world without consideration of the cultural values and national identity that this model would overrun. And, in fact, it may not be honest to speak so nobly about development aid and our concern for others when the best that we have proposed yet—for example the Alliance for Progress— stipulates a maximum growth rate for the third world of 2.5 percent per year, while it is considered essential that we grow a minimum of 4.5 or 5 percent. In other words, our very humanitarian efforts are based on a premise that we must grow richer faster than the poor. One might conclude that we were concerned primarily with the maintenance of our own superior position and only secondarily with the development of others or the development of markets.

Paul Ehrlich, in a small book called *The Population Bomb* states that we cannot remain affluent and isolated. At the moment the United States uses well over half of all the raw materials consumed in the world each year. That is, less than one-fifteenth of the population of the world requires more than all the rest to maintain its inflated position. And if present trends continue, Ehrlich says, in twenty years the United States will contain less than one-fifteenth of the population, and yet may use some eighty percent of the resources consumed. And he asks whether other countries, many of them in the grip of starvation and anarchy, will happily continue to supply these materials to a nation that cannot give them food?

In other words, if we express our concern about ecology, natural resources, acute misery, the future of man, population control, and our responsibility to the poor, without working for a radical transformation of those economic and political structures that maintain our affluence in the face of their poverty, we are nothing but blind hypocrites. No amount of population control is of itself going to alter social structures. On the contrary it would not be surprising if our eager efforts to reduce

76

population growth among the poor were really primarily efforts to reduce the size of a revolutionary army that will one day rise and seize our wealth.

There is another form of cultural imperialism in our talk about family planning. Mrs. Hussein has already pointed this out. What do we mean by family? Is our public concept of a family really more, even in our own culture, than a sentiment, an ideological illusion. What are we saying to the fatherless, the husbandless, the unmarried girl when we talk about family planning? Are we forcing our values and our terms upon others who may not accept our atomistic concept of the family and for whom North American individualism is essentially abhorrent? If we really care about human welfare and the social good, it seems to me. that we must speak about human communities and personal integrity without prejudging the issue by what we call the family. If we want to impose our cultural forms such as the family, then let us be honest and do it directly. If we believe in the right of people to decide whether or not they are to have children, then let us help them to have this choice regardless of the family question.

Through all of this runs another basic question. That is the nature of man himself. Is man, as so much of our talk assumes, essentially a consumer, or is man a creator and a producer as both the Old and the New Testaments claim? And if man is simply a consumer, then I would suggest we are probably on the right track already and we needn't bother much with the questions that I have been raising. But if man is more than a consumer, then we must deal with a host of questions about the quality and style of life. Then it is reasonable to suggest that we could shut down, for example, the entire automotive industry in Canada and use that productive facility to meet the real human needs of the entire world. Just look what could be done with the advertising budgets alone. During the summer of 1968 it was stated in the Toronto Globe and Mail that in this past year Chrysler spent $2,294,000 on advertising, Ford spent $3,500,000, American Motors spent $1,500,000, and General Motors spent $9,000,000 on advertising alone. And we say we can't do other things!

If our concern with population and resources would admit such a possibility as I am suggesting, then we might make Canada the primary producer of transportation systems. One consequence of this might be a reduction in air pollution, but more direct consequences would be the production of the kind of agricultural machinery the underdeveloped countries really need to improve their labour-intensive agriculture. It might mean the development of transportation that would enable people to get foodstuff to market while still fresh, and would open new areas for settlement and production and so forth. If we are not going to consider such an alternative then I think we should cease discussion altogether.

If our concern is really for the human family and for its future, then I think we have to push the discussion another step along the way, and ask if we can really meet human needs within the context of our present economic and political structures, based as they are, whether we like it or not, on the exploitation of the many for the benefit of a few. You need only look at the structures of the extractive industries in this country and abroad. If we are serious then I think we must seek a population limitation within a context of a vast and profound restructuring of the world economy and the distribution of wealth and control. If we are not willing to consider this, then our motives are not above suspicion, and imperialism might be a fair accusation.

Robert Heilbroner stated this case succinctly in the September, 1968, issue of *Harper's* when he stated that money is, unfortunately, the last if not the least step in the development sequence. For the long step out of backwardness is not merely a matter of getting richer but is first and foremost a matter of changing an entire society in ways that must go to the roots of its ordinary life, ways that are bound to shake or topple its basic structure of power and prestige. Our eager endorsement of technology as the cure for underdevelopment reveals all too clearly our failure to understand the social environment in which the process of change takes place. For example, the new seeds of rice or corn in India and Latin America were first used by the richer peasants; the poor ones cannot afford even to experiment for fear of starvation if the experiment fails, or simply because, being poor, they are the least ready for change, and as a result the disparity in income between the upper stratum of peasants and the lowest widens. To be sure there is more food but there is also more social misery.

If we are not willing to face the prospect and to work for radical social change, then I think we must face the alternative of controlling the numbers of the poor on the one hand and holding off the revolution by slightly easing causes of disquiet on the other. But if the values we are really concerned with have to do with human liberation, equality of opportunity, meaningful work, conservation of resources, open structures, and a healthy environment; if we see people as producers and creators, not merely as consumers: if these are our values then I think we might begin our analysis of the world's ills, not be looking at many isolated facets of the situation, not by looking first at the basic pattern of availability and distribution of resources, and at political control, and then at population size and growth, social structures and aspirations, and the overall life style and quality. Clearly it is not for us alone to decide the future of man, nor am I calling for any kind of isolationism, but it may be high time we stopped imposing our cultural values, our fears and our notions of good on everyone who would submit gratefully or not to our humanitarian efforts.

Clearly the time of imperialism is coming to an end, and it remains for us to fight the affluent and the powerful, to allow others to radically alter their life situations while we radically alter our own.

DISCUSSION FOLLOWING SECOND SESSION

Dr. Fidler:

Mr. Kneen has suggested that our interest in family planning in North America derives from our desire to retain control over the world economy or to hold off world revolution. How do the other speakers react to that statement?

Mrs. Hussein:

Did Mr. Kneen mean that attempts at promoting population control may be understood to be an imperialistic approach to reserve resources for the developed nations?

Mr. Kneen:

I suggest that if we were willing to look at our basic motivations, which could be of that sort, then the form of our discussion would change radically. You pointed to questions about the family which involve a lot of ideas which may not be acceptable to many North Americans who seem to be in favour of population control. At any rate such questions seem not to be a part of "population science."

Mrs. Hussein:

The feeling in our part of the world is that population control should involve more than family planning programmes. It is a much wider subject. Family planning in itself is valid from the point of view of family relationships and health and welfare of families, but it may never achieve the objective of population control unless other programmes are undertaken. Among these would be serious social and economic development, and such legislative acts as have been suggested by eminent sociologists like Kingsley Davis. In Egypt I think the idea that population control programmes are really motivated by imperialistic people has definitely been dropped. This may have been the attitude some time ago but now we are prepared to look at any possible solution in any direction, and we do have good will towards those people who recommend programmes for population control.

Mr. Kneen:

Mrs. Hussein has implied that in Egypt they assign a certain value to a programme within their own culture and then ask for assistance to meet that goal. That goal may coincide with what we think is good or it may not. Are we willing to supply assistance to people who request it when we don't agree with their choice of goal?

Miss Callwood:

Mrs. Hussein referred to the liberation of women. One of the factors that has given the human male great concern is that a woman is capable of being a sexual partner constantly while a man is limited by nature to some degree. It must have occurred to men in some distant early times that if women could get away with it they would copulate all the time; so they have taken great pains throughout the history of civilization to prevent women from doing this. But I think that recent history demonstrates that women who are free of the risk of pregnancy are not in general notably promiscuous. They apparently seem to be rather decent human beings anyway. We point this out to the kind of hysterical men that make laws controlling what happens to our ovaries. If they want to make laws like that, they should have ovaries for a while and then we would see what sort of laws they would write.

Questioner:

Dr. Dupré, you talked about the idea of intellectual integrity as the determining factor in making a decision on birth control. Is not this in fact really a myth and are not millions of people led to believe that intellectual integrity is not at all a determining factor? You also talked about personal conscience. Does not the Encyclical itself by its very existence make an utter mockery of the idea of personal conscience? Is it not artificial for you to say that individual conscience is the final determinant when millions of Catholics are taught that they must accept this verbatim? The question of intellectual integrity is not communicated to them at all and the results are personal neuroses, conflicts, etc. In other words, do not thinking Catholics have a responsibility for the Pope's action, a responsibility to stand up and say: "This is wrong"? By taking a neutral stand, are you really shirking that responsibility?

Dr. Dupré:

I think this is not a question, it is an objection, and I think it's a well-founded one. It is obviously the case that we in the Catholic Church, no matter what we say about this, have over long periods of time simply ignored this subjective factor of conscience of which I spoke in my talk. I am not going to deny this; it is absolutely true. I also think that the way this new document has been enforced, most notably in my own diocese of Washington where one priest is being suspended after another, is really frustrating the traditional doctrine that conscience is the ultimate norm. This confirms the objection that was made by the questioner and I entirely agree with that.

On the other hand, the fact that there is guidance, and guidance which for a Catholic is authoritative to some extent, does not necessarily take away intellectual integrity or freedom of conscience as long as you are aware of the limits of this guidance. But to say in general that any kind of document that you don't like takes away your intellectual integrity or freedom of conscience would not be entirely consistent. Are your moral norms exclusively determined by a process of reasoning? Is it not the case that most of our conclusions in moral matters, as in most other matters, are reached by way of information which we accept on the authority of someone else? Whether the information is true or false raises a problem which you have to decide for yourself, and this problem becomes particularly sticky if the information comes from a source which to you, for some reason, is particularly authoritative and which you accept with more respect, more reverence than normal sources of information. But it is our obligation to be aware of the limitations of these things and that is what I considered to be my task here.

It was not my purpose to say whether some act is right or whether it is wrong, or to say that what the Pope said doesn't make any difference. This is not the issue. I have given talks on birth control for the last two years and I was the first one to write against the traditional position of the Catholic Church in this hemisphere in 1963. It is quite obvious where I stand on this matter; I have written about it many times. You may think, and you may be right in thinking, that whatever the Pope says in the Encyclical is just baloney. This is quite possible, but the simple fact of the matter is that the man wrote the Encyclical, and for many people Encyclicals are one of the forms of expression of an authority that they consider to be sacred. Now are you really justified on the basis of the fact that you cannot agree with one document, with which you don't have to agree in the first place, to throw out the whole role for authority as non-existent? If you would handle problems in such a drastic way, there wouldn't be much left to live for in general.

Questioner:
Mr. Kneen, isn't your demand that social change take precedence over the problem of population as Utopian and difficult of achievement as Miss Callwood's, which involved a sort of millenium of parental love based

on environmental change?

Mr. Kneen:

That question is often asked at this point in history. There are innumerable people who will argue with a good liberal conscience that we must continue with our welfare programmes because these are obvious, pressing human needs. But this leads to a preoccupation with immediate needs, and to ignore why these needs arose. So we have more jails, more hospitals, more correctional institutions, more policemen—and on it goes. We get so busy dealing with the consequences of our basic social structures that we forget to examine those basic structures that are creating the problems.

I find myself more concerned with the causes, so I come down on that side in this argument; and I think I will continue to do so until I see a lot more consideration of why there are poor in this society, instead of simply talking about what we are going to do about them now that we have them. I don't accept that perversion of the biblical statement that we will always have the poor with us and therefore we must keep them with us.

Maybe I do sound Utopian, but frankly I am fed up with the realists and with the people telling me what is possible and not possible. We have no idea whatsoever of what is in fact possible. Far greater is the problem of our own mentality; we can't conceive of any alteration in our own selves or our own situations.

Questioner:

Miss Callwood, are not the "warm" mothers the real problem in our human population explosion?

Miss Callwood:

I don't see rushing out and mending other peoples' houses when your own roof is leaking. I suggest our gravest concern in North American society is for protection of the young against this gross maltreatment that comes not from just the parental inability to love but from the environment of poverty and deprivation. We should take care of this, simultaneously helping if a mother anywhere wants to have a baby and raise the baby. I don't see counting their noses and saying: "Now you have had three; you have had your quota and we are going to sterilize you." I take the Utopian point of view that if a woman wants to use her body to have babies, that's really great. She ought to be helped in every possible way to do it, whether she is black or green.

84

Questioner:

You have just been talking about the ideal approach. Certainly the warm mother is the ideal mother. But I repeat the question: Isn't she our greatest problem in trying to prevent a population explosion?

Miss Callwood:

I don't see her as a problem. We just have to feed her babies, that's all. We can do that I am sure, technologically. We can feed her babies and find something for them to enjoy life with.

Mrs. Hussein:

Maybe the questioner has in mind the developing countries where a good number of women, perhaps the majority, want to have children for one reason or another: What do you do about them? That is the dilemma that is faced by our family planning programme. There has to be an educational programme to produce social change if that can be done at all. There are various means of changing people's values through adult education. I don't think the majority of women would want to go on just having children.

Questioner:

Dr. Dupré, I would like to point out that in poor undeveloped countries with large Catholic populations the majority of the poor who are Catholic can't exercise the feelings of their conscience and use their intellectual integrity because they don't have any intellectual integrity. Secondly, in recent months the clergymen who have criticized the Encyclical and exercised their intellectual integrity have been pressured by the Episcopate and the Vatican to withdraw their opinions. To me the Pope's Encyclical says the salvation of the Catholic soul is more important than the continued existence of the majority of humanity. How can the Church justify the salvation of the Catholic soul against destruction of the majority of humanity?

Dr. Dupré:

There are really two questions here. The first one was a statement that underdeveloped people have no intellectual integrity. The questioner must have meant that there is no point in speaking about intellectual integrity when a person doesn't have a sufficiently developed intellect to reach the point where integrity or non-integrity becomes a problem. That is true, but that is not their fault, nor is it even the Catholic Church's fault. This is just the way things are, and this places heavy responsibilities on the pastoral, religious, and moral leaders of these people. The second point concerns clergymen who have been speaking in the way in which I have spoken, and have been asked to shut up by their bishops and by the Vatican. This statement is only true in a limited way. In some countries clergymen have been very much encouraged by their bishops to speak up in this particular way. What you state is true in my own diocese of Washington, D.C., and it's very sad. I think the majority of the diocese revolted against the attitude of the Bishop who took a stand which was not in conformity with accepted Catholic doctrine. If you want me to answer who was right from a traditional point of view, the answer is obviously the dissenting clergy. So if the word heresy is going to be thrown around, apply it to the Bishop and not to the clergy.

What about the statement that the Pope is only concerned about saving Catholic souls and letting the rest of the world go to pot? In this Encyclical, *Humanae Vitae*, and also in the previous one, *Populorum Progressio*, there is a strong emphasis on family planning. In fact in *Populorum Progressio* it is made very clear that not only the parents but also government leaders have a positive obligation in keeping the population under control. So to say that the Pope is saving the Catholic souls and ignoring the rest of the world is not true. For Catholics, there is a moral obligation. One can disagree with the Encyclical on whether the solutions which the Pope proposes for Catholics are the right ones, whether they are sufficient, whether they put undue hardship on Catholic couples. This is a valid question, but not whether the Pope is in favour of birth control or is against it. He is in favour of it. He has said that several times. The Encyclical concerns the kinds of birth control.

Finally, the Pope did not write his Encyclical for non-Catholics. He wrote it for Catholics and he has a hard enough time getting it accepted by some Catholics. So you don't have to worry about it influencing non-Catholics directly.

Questioner:
Mr. Kneen, if we are going to concentrate our attention on the quality of life, then I think we are unavoidably going to come up against a confrontation between authoritarian imposition of regulations which the word population control implies and your individual decision-making. If we have a population that is both breathing and polluting the air, then there is an imposition by some people on other peoples' freedom. Miss Callwood's policy of unrestricted birth by mothers who want children could not apply indefinitely; regulation of some form or another would have to be undertaken.

Mr. Kneen:

There is the question of who does the regulation. The problem of how we make informed public decisions is something we have hardly dealt with or even thought about. We have assumed in questions of family size that there are two people who know best and we have let them take care of it. I am calling that into question, because what this process has produced is not all that admirable. In fact it has led us to some rather sad situations, and sadder for others at this point than for ourselves.

One of the problems is that we continue to think in terms of the individual versus the state, which is a paraphrase of what you said. I am not sure that we can make any headway by approaching problems in this way. That kind of polarization is dehumanizing in itself, since man exists only in a community as a social being. Until we figure out what that means in terms of social structure, decision-making and authority, we cannot deal with specific questions.

There are a lot of women who would rather not have children, as well as those who would like to have children. There are those who are good at having children, and those for whom it is not a good thing for physiological, psychological, or other reasons. I suspect that if there were not so much pressure for social conformity a lot of people would not have children. Who says that the role of wife and mother is natural for every woman? There may be some women who can contribute far more to the human scene by remaining single, and the question of celibacy is quite unrelated to the first question. Until we open up the social structures to permit people to practise personal integrity and fulfil their desires as human beings, we don't know what is going to happen when we let people who want children have all they want, and don't force children on people who don't want them.

Dr. Fidler:

I think that there is ample evidence that women all over the world do want to exercise the ability to control procreation. Having in mind Mr. Kneen's concern about the imperialism of population control, I note that here in Canada we hide behind the Criminal Code to avoid responding to requests for assistance that come to our government from other governments who are actively engaged in providing women with this opportunity. In the light of Dr. Dupré's final statement in his presentation, to the effect that Catholics ought to cooperate actively in population control, I wonder how he suggests that the average Roman Catholic will get this message in Canada so that something will happen here?

Dr. Dupré:

This is a matter of strategy and I have always been notoriously bad in that. It seems to me that Catholics, for the time being, should concentrate on what they can do and what they should do rather than on questions on which they are going to be hopelessly divided. At this point it is a hopeless question to ask: "Is the Encyclical right or is it wrong?" That's why I didn't want to address that question. By arguing this question we simply divide the Catholic block more and more and as a result no action is going to be taken. Why don't we agree on the things which we must agree on? One of these things is that we have a responsibility that we must not ignore for those people who also have an obligation to respect their consciences. If respect for other people's conscience implies that one should not prevent them from doing what their conscience inspires them to do in their needs, it also obliges us to cooperate to help them to do what they should do according to their consciences. Why don't we concentrate on these problems?

If we want to, we can simultaneously maintain everything that is said in the Encyclical and at the same time mount a Catholic attack against a government prohibition of foreign aid in the form of birth control. In Canada I think that Catholics should be the first to do so because they are suspected of being the reactionary force; they should work hardest to get these laws off the books. Even the ones who accept the Encyclical should not feel that to do so would imply an anti-Encyclical attitude. What it really boils down to is that the basic attitude of the Catholic has been this: "Allright, that's not our problem; let someone who is not a Catholic do it." It was the attitude of the Catholic doctor in the past; when a woman would come for birth control advice he would just say: "Why don't you go next door? The doctor in the office next door to mine is a non-Catholic and can give you all the information." This silly nonsense ought to stop.

We have to meet our own responsibility and to tell people how they can act according to their conscience. And we should be the first, even by our own inefficient methods, in practising the principles of the Encyclical. We may produce more children than are needed, so we should be all the more anxious to provide possibilities for birth control to people who need them. Catholics have an additional obligation here of charity that the rest of the population might be less concerned about. We should be in the forefront of this action.

Questioner:

Mr. Kneen, while I am in complete accord with your idea of a Utopian framework and that we should examine our motivations when we are concerned about populations in other countries, I see that the population increases roughly by ten every five seconds. Surely this is a crisis of numbers and we have passed the point now where we can even take time to consider a Utopian viewpoint. It is an immediate problem.

Mr. Kneen:

How do you think we got here? We got into this situation because we refused to believe that there was anything to do other than to continue what we had already been doing. I think that's a rather poor way to proceed. To be Utopian really is to refuse to see what we are doing and what we really want. Then we get into the situation where we are always trying to deal with what has already happened. I have been involved in the Peace Movement for about ten years in one way or another. I got tired of marching in demonstrations against policies that were decided five years before by the Pentagon. When do we begin to say let's deal with the agenda we really want to deal with, instead of being reactionary all the time? The problem is increasing but to just go on handing out more bills and not look at the real problem isn't going to solve it either.

Questioner:

What I am saying is, haven't we passed the point where we can do that now? Shouldn't we do something almost right away while there is still a chance that something can be done about the problem?

Mr. Kneen:

I suggested that we could take the profit out of the manufacture of birth control devices now on sale, and make them available all over the place. Don't you think that would help? No one should have to ask anybody's permission to use them—just go ahead and do it.

Questioner:

Mrs. Hussein, could you discuss what precepts and teachings of the Koran and Islamic laws you saw as hindering efforts in the emancipation of women and family planning? Secondly, what do you think should be done to circumvent these hindrances?

Mrs. Hussein:

You apparently feel that I implicated the religion of Islam as being responsible for hindering women's emancipation. The problem involves the misinterpretation of the Islamic religion. There is a group of people in the country, mostly educated thinkers, who take the view that the Moslem religion is very progressive, especially from the point of view of the rights of women. For example, women have had the right to dispose of their

89

property independently of their husbands, to have an independent legal personality, to assume their maiden name after marriage, to undertake professions without permission of their husbands. These are indications that the religion was progressive with regard to the rights of women. Women had not been inheriting property before this religion came, about sixteen centuries ago. Women were even being buried alive at times, probably as one of the means of curtailing population growth in pre-Islamic days. Then a magic change took place in the position of women in the fact that they have come to be persons who would also become guardians over minors.

Over the years the religion has not been continuously interpreted in the right spirit. If the progressive interpretation of the religion were to be accepted now, I think that polygamy would definitely be abolished. Polygamy was accepted in its time as something of a necessity under existing conditions. For example, the Koran states that a man may marry one, two or four wives, on condition that he is fair to them, but he will not be fair to more than one no matter how hard he tries. It is a matter of interpretation. As early as the 1920's there were scholars who wanted to abolish polygamy. Somehow this has not been achieved in Egypt, though it has in Tunisia and Turkey.

The right of a man to divorce is something of a more serious nature. It used to be restricted to a certain extent by the solidarity of families. The family imposed its rules and regulations on married couples, and they would be resorted to for arbitration on a lot of matters, but this does not take place now. The woman does suffer from the fact that she can be repudiated unilaterally by the husband. We do not like to think that this was imposed by the religion as something that had to continue for centuries and centuries. We think that the theological part of the religion is different from the social legislative part and the latter should be adapted to the changing conditions.

In some ways Moslem legislation has been adapted to changing conditions in other areas than family law in Egypt. The penalty for theft, for example, used to be cutting off the hand, and this has been done away with. Even the penalty for adultery was different from what it is now. So if it has been proven that we can change Moslem legislation in the interests of society, I hold our present society and not the religion responsible for not making the move. As for family planning, the religion has never been an impediment.

THIRD SESSION

PROGRAMMING FOR SURVIVAL

IDEOLOGY, FAITH, AND FAMILY PLANNING IN LATIN AMERICA

Joseph Mayone Stycos

Joseph Mayone Stycos was born in New York State in 1927. He studied economics as an undergraduate at Princeton, then sociology for his Ph.D. at Columbia, and followed this with post-doctoral work at the University of North Carolina. He held professorial positions, each for a number of years, at the University of Puerto Rico and St. Lawrence University before moving to Cornell where he is now Chairman of the Department of Sociology.

Professor Stycos has done sociological and demographic research in a number of Latin America countries since 1950. He has published many papers on this and related subjects and has written or edited about ten books. Titles of the latter include "The Family and Population Control" in 1959, "The Control of Human Fertility in Jamaica" in 1964, and "Human Fertility in Latin America: Sociological Perspectives" in 1968.

Dr. Stycos has acted as consultant to many important private, national, and international agencies and has been a member on a variety of committees concerned about aspects of human population numbers.

The paradox of population in Latin America lies in the culture's inability to organize its immense land area and its considerable natural resources for the benefit of its relatively *small* population. This inability has deep roots in the past, and has many economic and political sustaining causes in the present which will not concern us here. However, given a social structure which generates economic growth with painful slowness, then the extremely rapid contemporary rates of population growth can be viewed only as an expensive luxury. If a nation *wishes* to emphasize quantity over quality, or to expend its resources disproportionately on the production of people rather than on the improvement of their well-being, then this is that nation's business. But what I wish to make clear is that at the present time and in the present state of social organization, most Latin Americans must confront such alternatives. Our task today is to see to what extent religious and political ideologies are obscuring the appreciation of this basic fact.

91

The Myth of Machismo. Low income populations in Latin America have high fertility. This is the fact, but the common explanation of this fact by intellectuals of both North and Latin America has tended toward the attribution to the lower classes of deep-rooted psychological drives for reproduction.

Even such a normally sober journalist as James Reston seems to lose control when dealing with the tantalizing concept of *machismo*, a tendency, according to Reston, which stems from the "stubborn vanity and stupidity of the ignorant male in Latin America . . . (who is) worse than the baboon and worships the cult of virility long after he has forgotten the cult of Christianity . . . The Latin male is not satisfied with love, he must have life—one new life a year, if possible, in order to prove he is good for something."[1]

The consequences of accepting such theories are not trivial, for the resistance of the baboon to social change is well-known. If big families are truly desired to prove virility, or, on the part of the female, to demonstrate womanliness, then provision of family planning services would be a waste of time and resources—an attitude which is still not uncommon in Latin America. In fact, public opinion surveys in Latin America show that men and women there are not so simple-minded as we would have them. On the average they want three or four children. If some of you think this is a large family, you just do not know enough about baboons.

In the absence of public discussion of the question, and in the light of general ignorance about the "controllability" of human fertility, we should not expect women's attitudes to be intense, well-crystallized, and unswerving. But at the same time there is little doubt that there is a latent preference for a moderate family size rather than for a large one.

There are at least three things which can be done with such a latent preference: (1) we may leave it as it is and make the technology so easy that little more motivation is required; (2) we may wait for the latent preference to become activated "naturally" as a product of social and economic changes that will alter aspiration levels; (3) by means of direct education it may be reinforced, crystallized, and intensified to the extent that the individual will act.

The "great debate" today is between the latter two alternatives. In the scientific world, the hypothesis that the demographic transition can be achieved by means of direct educational techniques is typified by Donald Bogue, who maintains that "Family planning research . . . begins with the assumption that by discovery of new principles we may be able to devise programs that can accomplish the desired results more quickly than would be possible if we waited for the solution along the lines of increased literacy—rising urbanization, improved levels of living, increased contact with technological-cultural change."[2] We should note that Bogue is not only propounding a theory of social change, but an *ideology*. It is not surprising that it collides with at least one other combined theory of social change and action ideology—Marxism.

Ideological Conflict. Throughout most modernizing countries, and especially in Latin America, we can distinguish at least three major ideological types—the conservative, the social reformist, and the revolutionary. The conserative puts the status quo first and revolution last with social change a reluctant second place. The reformer puts social change first and the status quo last, with revolution occupying a second place. The revolutionary puts revolution first and social change last. He prefers the status quo to social change because the latter might stem the revolution, while the former, the more intolerable it becomes, can only precipitate it.[3]

Increasingly economists are of the opinion that population control can accelerate economic development by such means as decreasing the dependency ratio, reducing the cost of social services, decreasing unemployment and raising per capita product. In addition to spreading the benefits of economic development less thin, there should be positive generation of economic development as a result of increased savings for investments in capital producing enterprises. Finally, by alleviating food shortages and other pressures attributable to population increase (e.g., rural over-crowding and urban migration) social tensions might be eased. It should be noted that the gains from population control can occur without any basic changes in the economic and social structure, e.g., without any radical change in the distribution of wealth, ownership of the means of production, etc. Strictly rationally, population control should be of the highest priority to conservatives, of importance but secondary importance to social reformists, and anathema to revolutionaries.

As usual, the revolutionaries have reacted most consistently, and have resisted population control as another palliative of the social reformist ilk which will ease the pressures leading to revolution, diverting attention from the true source of society's ills—the capitalist economic system. More recently, some communist spokesmen have softened the traditional Marxian hostility to Malthusian theory to the extent of admitting that population growth can impede economic progress and that birth control can alleviate population growth. They feel that birth control, however, will be and *should be* a natural response to the necessary revolutionary changes in society. That Communist nations have some of the most efficient birth control programmes in the world, while condemning population control, is proof that they are not opposed to birth control *per se*, but only to the *ideology* of population control and to its proposed sequence in the development of societies.

The conservatives, who should be most enthusiastic about birth control, are split because of conflicting ideologies and credos. In Latin America they tend to be the more traditional and orthodox Catholics who may have moral objections to family planning, and they are also from the business world which sees more consumers and a cheap labour supply as the very fuel of industry. Finally, many conservatives are strongly nationalistic, and they view with pride a populous nation, regarding population control, as a new method of the colonial powers to emasculate the nations they hope to continue to dominate. Thus, the editor of El Salvador's *Diario de Hoy*, Napoleon Viera Altamirano, warns against "the true conspirators against our America, who come with a plan of massive destruction! They plan to destroy the capital of Latin America, to frighten away private investment, to socialize us before we have capitalized, and to block our growth, cutting the wombs of Latin mothers, castrating Latin males, before we have grown sufficiently or taken possession of the vast empty lands of the continent."[4]

In point of fact birth control is making greatest headway among the liberals or social reformers who are gradually becoming convinced that it can speed the economic development they desire without jeopardizing any of the social reforms they espouse. Of equal or even greater importance, they see birth control as a social measure, as a means of reducing abortion and illegitimacy, and as a way of increasing human freedom and control over man's nature. Since they tend to be nominal Catholics or leftist activist Catholics, moral-religious considerations are not of paramount importance. Their main preoccupation about family planning is with respect to its suspiciously enthusiastic promotion by the United States. The more they are convinced, by President Johnson and others, that five dollars invested in birth control is worth 100 dollars invested in economic development, the more concerned they are that the bargain-loving United States will choose the five-dollar investment. In addition, unaware that the conservatives are confused on the issue, they are afraid that both American and local conservatives will substitute Lippes loops for agrarian reform.

In sum, there is not only academic debate over whether or not direct education and services can bring down birth rates, there are definite ideological differences concerning its desirability, sequence, and overall place in the strategy of development.

Faith. In addition to ideology there is the area of faith, which I use here to refer to religious principles affecting the population issue. Although the Catholic Church has tended toward a pro-natalist ideology, its principal potential relation to population has stemmed from its faith in a natural law adjuring interference with the physiological consequences of

94

the sexual act.

In the past I have insisted on the irrelevance of this faith to contraceptive practice in Latin America, but the recent Papal Encyclical compels us to reconsider the question. What has been the reaction of Latin Americans to the Encyclical?

*The Hierarchy.*Unlike the storm of protest among North American and European prelates, the Latin American hierarchical reaction was relatively mild and orthodox, although few were as blasé as the Puerto Rican Churchman who announced that "the Encyclical should cause neither alarm nor confusion among Catholics."[5] Aside from being a political victory for the Church's conservative wing, the Encyclical was well-received among those who feel a tidal wave of hedonism is sweeping the world. A Costa Rican priest, in congratulating the Papal Nuncio, referred to the "unbraked sensualism and hedonism threatening the family and society," and maintained that the Encyclical had "again saved the world from ruin."[6] The Archbishop of Cuenca in Ecuador believes that it serves to "contain the demoralization of the family and conjugal life";[7] and a cable to the Pope from the Peruvian Bishop referred favorably to its defence of "married life against a reigning hedonism."[8] Most explicit of all was Colombia's Monsigneur Valencia Cano who held that "exhibitionism in all forms is making continence impossible, with the logical *sequelae* of homosexuality and the most aberrant bestiality . . . (These) excesses are most evident in the developed countries . . . (The) Encyclical is a violent but necessary brake to sexual corruption in the western world."[9]

A few spokesmen found it necessary to account for the Encyclical in supernatural terms. The Archbishop of Medellin, Colombia, announced that the decision must have been made "with the special assistance of the Holy Spirit,"[10] and the Secretary of the Colombian hierarchy explained further. "This document can only be understood," he announced, "in the light of the supernatural and theological significance of the *magisterio pontifico*. If we don't believe that the Holy Spirit illuminates the Pope, we will never be able to understand it."[11] Whenever directly asked, Churchmen noted that the Encyclical was not infallible, but it was not usual to make explicit, as did the Auxiliary Bishop of Montevideo, that it was "consequently reformable."[12] When caught with a direct question on whether the use of contraceptives would henceforth be a venial or mortal sin, an archbishop of Paraguay answered uneasily: "It is hard to say."[13] The Bishop of Cuernavaca recommended "careful study, in order to understand the precise teaching of the encyclical and the extent to which the faithful are bound by the norms that it expresses."[14] The hierarchy of the Dominican Republic also recommended a studious approach: "We ask all our beloved brethren," they said, "to study and meditate with the

95

greatest care and frankness of spirit the Encyclical *Humanae Vitae*."[15] But the Archbishop of Port-of-Spain, Trinidad, seemed the most desperate: "Continue saying your prayers, earnestly and sincerely," he urged, "and the all-powerful grace of God will undoubtedly come to your help."[16]

In a number of countries the Encyclical was turned against North American family planning programmes abroad. The Archbishop of Tegucigalpa, Monsigneur Héctor Enrique Santos, designated the family planning programme in Honduras as "totally immoral," and tending to "develop prostitution" in the nation. "A foreign government," he added, "which conditions its aid by programs of this kind is not a friend but an enemy which seeks to reduce us to permanent impotence."[17] In Costa Rica the Archbishop's Office took the opportunity to say: "It would be interesting to find out how many thousands of dollars have been invested in Costa Rica in that campaign of disorientation and disrespect for human dignity . . . Use of the pill or coil has been used as a condition for medical treatment or family assistance."[18] The Apostolic Administrator of Colombia, Monseigneur Muñoz Duque referred to United States aid on family planning as "a flagrant violation of the Rights of Man expressed in the United Nations Charter,"[19] while a Cartagena priest conceived a new form of political masochism. "Any nation accepting such (birth control) conditions," he said, "enslaves in man the freest act of nature."[20]

While outright opposition to the Encyclical was rarely expressed publicly, two exceptions in Brazil should be mentioned. The auxiliary Bishop of Porto Alegre and Secretary General of the National Bishops Conference, Dom Ivo Lorscheisder, flatly disagreed with the Encyclical and declared himself favourable to the contraceptive pill.[21] Even more spectacular were *Journal do Brazil's* large headlines on August 10 announcing, "DEBATE AMONG PRIESTS APPROVES PILL 4 TO 1". The discussion took place among several priests and physicians at the Conference of Brazilian Clergy (Religiosos) before an audience of 100 priests, friars, and secular Catholics. One priest called the text of *Humanae Vitae* totally obsolete, and a Benedictine physician, complaining about the Encyclical's lack of attention to the fertility problems of the individual, explained that "we cannot expect the Pope to solve (such problems)—he who spent five years finding out whether or not the pill should be swallowed." Dom Tito went on to solve some of these individual problems himself, and recommended to those whose consciences hurt that they "use the pill and practice periodic abstinence, thus giving each side its due."[22]

There is no doubt that debate goes on. Even in that mecca of conservative Catholicism, Medellin, Colombia, "young priests share the opinions of high Churchmen in Europe and Canada that the Encyclical was not what they had hoped for after the recommendation of the special papal Commission," while "older priests stick firmly to the text and point out the grave sin of those who use artificial contraceptives."[23] Increasingly, however, we may anticipate attempts on the part of the conservative clergy to eliminate such controversy, at least from the public view. Thus, Cardinal Jaime de Barros Camara of Brazil in mid-August forbade public statements on the part of clergy "criticizing, contradicting, negating, or teaching differently" Papal policy on birth control.[24] But in the future there will perhaps be more accentuation of the positive, as manifested in the conclusion of the Latin American Assembly of the Christian Family Movement. In addition to categorizing the Encyclical as neither "irreformable nor infallible," they say something new and unusual about it: "For the first time," they pointed out, "an Encyclical is presented as a point of departure for subsequent reflection."[25]

Whatever the Church does, the ultimate question is what will Latin American Catholics do? Here we must divide our attention between the middle classes, who, by and large, are already controlling their fertility, and the lower classes, who are not. In the former category we turn to the opinions of the educated woman, as noted in the Latin American press.

Middle Class Women. It is not customary in Latin America for the middle classes to preach what they practice, but the Encyclical gave them a rare opportunity for doing so, especially women. Women in professional occupations were particularly sought out by journalists since they were more newsworthy, articulate and since, as women, they were at last relevant to a public issue.

One of the remarkable things brought to light was the willingness of middle and upper class women to speak up in public about the issue. They not only freely discussed contraception but freely disagreed with the Pope. Both these facts showed that there had been a revolution among Catholic women which the very Church had been instrumental in creating.

In Colombia, *El Tiempo* published the names, occupations, and photographs of their interviewees, and the illustrations below give the frank and aggressive flavour of the women's responses.[26] *Especially noteworthy is the high degree of awareness and concern for broad demographic problems.*

A Public Relations Expert: "It seems counterproductive . . . for years the university educated classes have been practicing family planning. In my case in ten years of marriage I have a boy of four and a girl of four months . . . "

A Secretary: "Many people will use their own methods and that's what I will do."

An Artist: "May the Holy Father, during his visit to an underdeveloped country such as ours, realize the poverty and the demographic problems common to all Latin America."

A Radio Announcer: "The necessity not only to plan the family but especially to slow down the demographic explosion is so obvious that it is difficult to explain why the Church made a decision which officializes a latent schism."

Those of you who are not familiar with the taboos on expression of these kind of sentiments in Latin America may not be as surprised as some of us who have seen a real revolution in the expression of these attitudes. I will read you one more.

Miss Bogota: "It seems ridiculous that the Church would pronounce against contraception in the way they have . . . We are in the midst of a terrible population explosion . . . For people without education it is very difficult to pretend that periodic continence is adequate."

The most fascinating interview, however, can best be described as semi-private. In Costa Rica, *La Republica's* reporter interviewed six professional women in a group, published their names and photographs, but did not attribute any particular quotation of any particular women.[27] The women were aware of these conditions and their comments seem even less inhibited than those cited above, and the atmosphere is more like a group discussion in a *private* situation. They begin by requesting "non-attribution" for two reasons:

"Most women are against the Encyclical, but as we're Catholics and part of a Catholic society, it hurts us to speak publicly against it; and in practice we can't accept what is being asked."

"Rhythm is permitted, but what can assure us a normal cycle? The pills. So we go back to pills to regularize menstruation? That's why the Encyclical is extremely difficult to explain. Too drastic!"

"The problem for the priest is tremendous. I'm a good Catholic and go to him when I need advice, but two weeks ago he allowed me to use the pills. Now what? Two weeks ago it wasn't a sin and now it is."

I do not pretend that these are systematic or scientific surveys, nor have I presented examples of the minority opinions favourable to the

Encyclical. I only wish to point out that when this many professional women are willing, in small countries with even smaller professional classes, to speak out publicly and semi-publicly with such intensity and frankness, it means that something real and important has happened to professional Latin American women in this decade, and that their freedom from certain ancient religious and sexual taboos is becoming a reality.

Lower-Class Women. What effect will the Encyclical have on the lower-class woman?—when she hears of it, that is. Two weeks after the Encyclical we asked a sample of 100 women attending out-patient clinics in Tegucigalpa, Honduras, whether they had heard about the Pope's new Encyclical. Ninety percent said they had not. Assuming our sample was haywire, we took a probability sample of 330 lower income urban homes, most of which have radio. Three to four weeks after the announcement of the Encyclical, only 20 percent of the women had heard of it. We asked those who had whether it had changed their thinking about family planning. Nine out of ten said no. Finally, we asked them whether it would change what they were *doing*. Half of them said no, nobody said yes, and the rest said they weren't doing anything.

We asked the women to tell us why they did not agree with the Pope, and here are some of the answers:

"The Pope is not God."

"The Pope does not know the true life of the poor."

"The Pope will not help us to raise our children."

"The real evil is to bring them to the world to suffer, or to die in abortion."

"I am a Catholic but I am also poor and it hurts to see my children without shoes, and naked."

Of course such women, already apparently well-motivated might be taught the periodic continence technique of birth control. If so, the clergy and/or the medical profession in Latin America will have time for nothing else. Let me give you two examples from Colombia, where Catholic groups have been attempting to communicate the rhythm technique over the past two years.

In an urban setting, in Bogota, the Jesuit University's family planning clinic at the San Ignacio Hospital held 2,900 private consultations over the past two years. In addition, 15 short courses reached 1,276 women. These led to 1,870 patients who enrolled and were given initial instructions. What was the net result? Their current report shows 133 women classified on rhythm.[28]

An even more intensive effort was made at the El Guabal Clinic in Cali. By the end of 1966 they had had 2,393 medical consultations, 5,642 auxiliary nurse home visits or interviews, 2,324 social worker home visits or interviews, and 188 group meetings. The result? "188 couples on rhythm—or 56 contacts per effective couple."[29]

Conclusions. While it is too early to tell what the effects of the Encyclical will be, they appear to be more at the programmatic and political levels than at the level of the individual conscience, but even here it is only a matter of time before public demand will compel governments to supply family planning services. It may also only be a matter of time before the Catholic Church adjusts to the new facts of life, and before the leftists abandon their encouragement of more misery as the shortest road to revolution or reform. But time or timing, after all, is the most which most of us can hope to affect—to speed up some things and to slow others down. In Latin America, as in many parts of the world, to slow the rate of population growth is to speed its rate of economic development; by the same token to speed its rate of economic growth is ultimately to slow its rate of population growth. But to say that the two are mutually related is not to say that they are equally important, for the slowing of population growth is a means toward the end of economic development. Nor can population control solve the problems of starvation, crime on the streets, and political unrest. Thre is no simple solution to any of our major problems today, because our major problems today are not simple.

But, as I hope I have shown, neither is the problem of population control simple, surrounded as it is by ideological controversy, questions of religious faith, and suspicions of political domination. In the light of these delicate considerations *the internationalization of population control programmes* becomes of the highest priority. At the present time the North American foreign aid programme and the North American foundations and private international agencies such as the International Planned Parenthood Federation carry the brunt of the programmes, by default, since the international governmental programmes are painfully weak. The United Nations continues to provide superb demographic analytical services, but it is unequipped to handle the pressing needs in population programming. The Organization of American States is grappling effectively with the problems of relating economic and social planning to population problems, but it cannot venture into technical assistance programmes since these are logically the province of Pan-American Health Organization, an organization whose impressive paper programme in family planning is innocent of organization, staff, or conviction. While international agencies cannot set goals for nations, they can assist nations in reaching for these goals. Thus, if Argentina, after weighing the pros and cons, wishes to speed up its rate of population growth, such an agency should help it to do so; but if Honduras wishes to slow down its rate of growth it should also help it. No Church, no creed, no ideology should or probably could stand in the way of this approach to national interests.

As for the Church, let me speak to those theologians and members of the hierarchy whose response to the Encyclical was that it opened the way for further thought and study. Please do both of these things. For Christianity has for so long provided us with a negative morality for our sexual lives that it is unprepared for an era of positive sexuality. This is perhaps the last chance the Christian Churches will have for a meaningful unity. It is a challenge to go beyond the abstract cliches of "responsible parenthood," a challenge to rise above the level of plastic and pills, a challenge to do something constructive with the power the Christian Churches have left.

1. – *New York Times*, April 9, 1967.

2. – Donald J. Bogue, "Family Planning Research: An Outline of the Field," in *Family Planning and Population Programs*, ed. B. Berelson, *et al*. (Chicago: Chicago University Press, 1966), p. 724.

3. – See Albert O. Hirschman, *Journeys Toward Progress* (New York: The Twentieth Century Fund, 1963), pp. 276-97.

4. – *Diario de Hoy* (El Salvador), June 21, 1963, cited in J.M. Stycos, "Opinions of Latin-American Intellectuals on Population Problems and Birth Control," *Annals of the American Academy of Political and Social Sciences*, CCCLX, pp. 45-6.

5. – Father Jaime Capo, Reported in *El Mundo* (San Juan), July 31, 1968.

6. – Apostolic Administrator of Alajuela Diocese, reported in *La Republica* (San Jose), August 3, 1968.

7. – *El Comercio* (Quito), August 17, 1968.

8. – *El Espectador* (Bogota), August 3, 1968.

9. – *El Tiempo* (Bogota), August 8, 1968.

10. – *El Siglo* (Bogota), August 3, 1968.

11. – *El Espectador* (Bogota), August 30, 1968.

12. – *El Universal* (Caracas), August 3, 1968.

13. – *El Espectador* (Bogota), August 20, 1968.

14. – *New York Times*, August 8, 1968.

15. – *Listin Diario* (Santo Dominog), August 1, 1968.

16. – *Trinidad Guardian* (Port-of-Spain), August 10, 1968.

17. – *El Dia* (Tegucigalpa), August 19, 1968.

18. – *La Republica* (San Jose), July 31, 1968.

19. – *El Espectador* (Bogota), August 1, 1968.

20. – *Ibid.,* August 8, 1968.

21. – *Jornal do Brasil* (Rio de Janeiro), August 17, 1968.

22. – *Ibid.,* August 10, 1968.

23. – *El Espectador* (Bogota), July 31, 1968.

24. – *Jornal do Brasil* (Rio de Janeiro), August 17, 1968.

25. – *El Espectador* (Bogota), August 27, 1968.

26. – *El Tiempo*, August 1, 1968.

27. – *La Republica*, August 11, 1968.

28. – Francisco Garcia-Conti, "Third Report on the Development of Family Planning Program and Research in the Physiology of Reproduction," Colombian Association of Medical Schools, May 1, 1967, mimeographed.

29. – Mario Jaramillo and Juan Lodoño, "Primera Valoracion Comparativa de los Servicios Pilotos de Planification Familiar," *Regulacion de la Fecundidad*, I, P. 43.

POPULATION
AND
PUBLIC HEALTH

Kamarazu Narasimha Rao

Kamarazu Narasimha Rao was born in Andhra Pradesh, India in 1907. He trained in medicine and then entered the military wing of the Indian Medical Service. Following post-graduate studies in London, England, he returned to India and the war in Asia. He was a prisoner-of-war in Singapore from 1942 to 1945.

After filling a number of senior administrative posts in Madras, Dr. Rao transferred to the Civil Branch of the Indian Medical Service. He was then active in various roles including superintendent of a tuberculosis sanitorium, professor of medical jurisprudence, professor of tuberculosis, and district medical officer. More recently he was Director of Medical Services of Andhra Pradesh, then Director-General of Health Services in India's Ministry of Health. In 1968 he was Visiting Professor of International Health at the University of Toronto.

Professor Rao has travelled widely since 1930. He has been a member of many committees, commissions and councils of the World Health Organization, UNICEF, and other organizations concerned with human health problems. His books and papers include "Nation's Health" in 1962, "Medical Manpower Needs for a Comprehensive Health Care in India 1966", and "The Indian Family Welfare Planning Programme in 1966".

Great discoveries have recently been made by man and of them the fission of the atom and the deciphering of the genetic code stand out prominently. Atomic power is yet to be used for peaceful purposes on a large scale for fighting the five giants, want, squalor, disease, ignorance, and idleness. It is hoped that the deciphering of the genetic code will open new horizons in the solution of the problems of population pressure and public health. When man invented agriculture 8,000 years ago, the agricultural revolution started, and it made possible the growth of populous human communities. With the gradual improvement of agricultural technology, production of surplus food was made possible to support those in the cities who worked in industry or trade or administered the state. The beginnings of urban revolution laid the foundation of civilization. But food supplies, on which depend the health of the people, have never been enough to maintain human populations. Today we see not only the world's food problem but also discern the biological, social, and economic changes required to solve it and attain a state of well-being, physical, mental, and social. In this paper I shall endeavour to discuss the problem of population, the health aspect of population dynamics, the work of the World Health Organization in this field and a programme in a developing country.

Population Trends and Their Effects

Man spread to most parts of the world a long time ago and in every part his numbers have increased. The million years of man on earth is divided into three periods: the first from almost one million B.C. to 6000 B.C.; the second from 6000 B.C. to 1650 A.D.; and the third from 1650 to modern times. Perhaps we may add a fourth period with the beginning of the Atomic Age. It is estimated that during the first period, which covered the old Stone Age to the beginnings of the new Stone Age, human population grew to about five millions, and the birth rate was close to 50 per 1,000. During the second period which included the new Stone Age (6000 B.C. to 3000 B.C.), through the Bronze Age, (3000 B.C. to 2000 B.C.), and the Iron Age (2000 B.C. to 600 A.D.), through Classical Antiquity and the Dark Ages, the Renaissance and Reformation, it is estimated that the world population grew from five million to half a billion. The third period (1650 to modern times) brought a six-fold increase in human numbers, from 500 million to three billion.

The determinants of increase of population are biological, social, and economic; and by and large the degree of operation of the Malthusian triad—war, famine and pestilence—and artificial fertility control appear to be important factors in limiting the increase.

The growth of populations depends on birth rates being in excess of death rates. When birth rates are constant and death rates are reduced by control or eradication of disorders, populations increase. If opportunity for migration to different lands is available the population increase is greater. When, along with the fall in death rates, birth rates are reduced by artifical fertility control measures the populations remain steady or grow moderately. The differential infant mortality, the general mortality and its causes, and the expectation of life all give indication of the factors operating in different socio-economic groups in different countries.

A study of the demographic cycle indicates that populations in countries go through five phases. In the first phase death rates and birth rates are high and stationary. In the second death rates decline but birth rates continue to be high. In the third the death rates decline further and although birth rates also tend to fall the rate of population increase is high. In the fourth phase approximate stability is reached and both birth and death rates are kept low. In the fifth the fall in birth rate is so great that population, despite low death rates, declines. This phase is largely hypothetical since only one country, France, has ever reached it and even this country is rapidly changing and returning to the fourth phase. It is calculated that to assure replacement, each couple who produce children should have on the average about 2.2. With this the net reproduction rate would be about 1.0 which represents a fertility rate just high enough to keep the population constant.

The population of 3,551 million (mid-1969) is unevenly distributed over the world.[1] Europe is densely populated (456 million or 12.8 percent) as are parts of Asia—East Asia (906 million or 25.5 percent), South Asia (1,156 million or 32.5 percent)—together more than half the human world. Northern North America (225 million or 6.3 percent), Oceania (19 million or 0.5 percent), U.S.S.R. (241 million or 6.8 percent), Latin America (276 million or 7.8 percent) and Africa (344 million or 9.7 percent), all have less dense populations.

The ten countries with the largest populations are ranked as follows, showing also the percent that each contributes to the world population: China (21), India (15), U.S.S.R. (7), U.S.A. (6), Pakistan (4), Indonesia (3), Japan (3), Brazil (2), West Germany (2), United Kingdom (2).

The annual percent rates of increase in different areas of the world are: World, 1.9; Africa, 2.4; Northern North America, 1.1; Middle America, 3.3; Temperate South America, 1.7; South West Asia, 2.4; Middle South Asia, 2.7; South East Asia, 2.2; East Asia, 1.5; Europe, 0.8; Oceania, 1.8; U.S.S.R. 1.0; Canada, 2.0. With the present rate of growth the percentages of populations of countries will vary in time A United Nations source (*Unesco Courier*, February, 1965) predicts on the continuing recent trends a population for the world of 7,410 million in 2000 A.D.

With the advent of modern public health movement and success in prevention of communicable diseases, etc., the population growth in many developing countries in the second and third phases of the demographic cycle is likely to continue so high as to become a public health problem.

It may be observed that a stage has been reached in the demographic development of the world when the rate of human reproduction in any part of the globe may directly or indirectly affect the health and welfare of the rest of the human race. It is in this sense that the social scientists consider that there is a world population problem.

Public Health Aspects of Population Dynamics

The relationship of population to health is a vital one. Health in any social group depends upon the dynamic relationship between numbers and the space they occupy, whether in a dwelling, town, city, neighbourhood or nation, and the education and training they have received for their needs. Public health, therefore, is concerned with demography: size of population, its distribution, the age structure, birth and death rates in specific age groups and socio-economic groups, and migration.

The morbidity in the lower socio-economic groups, as revealed by health surveys, is much higher than in the higher income groups who practice fertility control. The infant mortality and general mortality is much higher again in the lower income groups than in the affluent. It is also noted that over-population and over-crowding affect the community physically and mentally. In developing countries and in the lower socio-economic groups on the poverty line with over-crowding there is greater sickness. Winslow[2] in his brilliant book shows that men and women are sick because they are poor; they become poorer because they are sick; and sicker because they are poorer.

It is estimated that more than two-thirds of the world's population is suffering from under-nutrition and malnutrition, with less than 2,000 calories per person per day. The areas of greatest deficiency are Central America, Africa, Asia, and the Middle East. Poor nutrition predisposes to infection. Malnutrition is perhaps the chief cause of high death rates from preventable diseases, low life expectancy, high mortality in infancy and childhood. With increasing food shortages and declining mortality due to control of communicable diseases, malnutrition and under-nutrition have added to the population crisis. In the *World Food Survey* published by the Food and Agricultural Organization (1946), it was pointed out that "Poverty is the chief cause of malnutrition. It is interesting to observe that all the countries in which the supply of calories per caput was less than 2,250 a day were countries in which the average per caput income was less than 100 U.S. dollars a year."

Gunnar Myrdal in his address at the Fifth World Health Assembly (1952) clearly outlined the theory of cumulative causation. If there is no socio-economic development concurrently with the decline in death rates, the lives so saved by the health programmes will only add to unemployment and consequent pauperization. The cycle of poverty and disease described by Winslow again comes to operate when there is a population pressure.

In the developing countries, not only is there a great shortage of

108

health manpower, but there is also lack of hospitals, clinics, and health centres, along with schools. The shortage of schools, hospitals, and other social services that are needed to cope with the increased population is a great impediment to progress, for even the existing populations have not been served with minimal services. The consequence, therefore, of population increase is overcrowding, with lowered standards of health and quality of service.

The urbanization that is taking place in developing countries in association with rural-urban migration of population leads to very unsatisfactory conditions of health. Studies in the social etiology of the health conditions reveal essentially the problems which arise from or are associated with inadequate water supplies and drainage, unhygienic housing conditions, lack of educational and recreational facilities.

In most of the developing countries, about 40 percent of the population is under the age of 15. The combination of rapid growth of population and heavy dependency presents major obstacles to modernization and the economic growth so vitally necessary for higher levels of living and health.

The effects of repeated pregnancies on maternal health deserves the greatest consideration. With malnutrition and under-nutrition, repeated pregnancies sap the mother's health, cause premature labour, abortions, anaemia, neglect of children, and the consequent adverse effects on the health and happiness of the family unit.

Maternal mortality due to induced abortions is high in many countries. There is need to investigate the causes of maternal death to determine the causes and take preventive measures. Infant mortality in the low socio-economic groups is high largely because of nutritional disorders and poor environmental conditions. Inefficiency in reproduction and inability to care properly for the young indicate the need for spacing of pregnancies so that there may be recuperation of maternal health and individual attention for each child. There is a need, therefore, for a preventive approach to maternal mortality, abortions, and infant and child mortality.

Mental health is in great jeopardy because of the hopelessness of life in circumstances where there exists neither shelter, food, well-being nor any basic opportunities to make fulfilment of the purpose of life possible. Because mental health and unwanted pregnancies and children are very much related, population size is a matter of concern to public health.

In 1967, WHO published its third report on the world health situation.[3] Many countries like India, Ceylon, China (Taiwan), Colombia, Thailand, etc., reported health problems created by the rapid growth of population and the pressure it exerts on the economic situation and on the standards of living. The report pointed out that "In some instances as in several island countries, geography is the activating force and in India the major factor is the *massive size of its population*."

Apart from the high annual rate of natural increase, the problems of immigration and the consequent public health aspects have to be kept in view. Immigrants into Hong Kong, West Germany, Switzerland, and India have created health problems in association with pressure on housing accommodation, sanitary services, water supplies, etc. Other social services such as educational facilities are over stretched. Age and sex of the immigrants, particularly males in the age group 20-24, create special problems. These population movements are invariably associated with the immigration-urbanization-industrialization complex.

Many countries are turning to comprehensive health planning. Population parameters have to be taken into account in estimating the needs of health services both quantitatively and qualitatively in response to population trends. There is need to develop the basic infrastructure of health services in which maternal and child health are integrated, as child-bearing patterns are deeply influenced when health measures give greater assurance that children will survive. Health factors and health services are thus important components of the equations that determine population trends. There is an intimate relationship between maternal and child health and such factors as age at pregnancy, parity, the spacing of children, foetal wastage and abortion, which speaks strongly for including services for sub-fertility, sterility, abortion, pregnancy, sexual education, etc. Family planning health services should keep in view the needs for operational research and for developing innovations in this area.

Role of the World Health Organization in this Field.

The World Health Assembly in its resolutions, W.H.A. 18.49, W.H.A. 19.43, W.H.A. 20.41 and W.H.A. 21, defined the organization's role in the area of family planning: "They enable the WHO to advise governments upon request in the development of health programmes concerned with family planning services." WHO does not endorse or promote any particular population policy, recognizes that problems of human reproduction involve the family unit as well as society, and that the size of the family is the *free choice of each individual family*.

As a result the organization has received requests from and has given advisory services to the Central African Republic, Kenya, Colombia, Costa Rica, El Salvador, Haiti, Honduras, Nicaragua, Trinidad and Tobago, Pakistan, India and Nepal, and the Republic of Korea. The organization lays great emphasis on training of personnel to deal with health aspects of human reproduction, family planning, and population dynamics.

110

WHO has also taken up research in the field of family planning and population dynamics including operational research. Epidemiological studies of the complications and health hazards arising from pregnancy under different social, economic, and cultural conditions are being taken up.

Problems of the side-effects and safety aspects of fertility regulating agents are considered by WHO as of particular importance, as they involve large numbers of women in the reproductive age group. "The possible hazards of contraceptive agents have to be weighed against the potential benefits to family health for couples desiring fertility regulation as well as the potential hazards of maternal morbidity secondary to unwanted pregnancies and abortion."

The WHO[4] has further convened over ten meetings of expert committees and scientific groups to deal with hormone steroids in contraception, and the physiological and clinical aspects of intra-uterine devices and other related problems.

The organization is currently collaborating and coordinating its activity in this field with several other agencies of the UN system.

Programmes in Some Developing Countries.

There is a governmental concern in many countries. Besides the great interest shown in this field by developed countries, a large number of governments of developing countries have taken up active programmes. Some of them are India, Pakistan, Korea, Taiwan, Thailand, Tunisia, Turkey, Egypt, Brazil, Chile, Colombia, Venezuela.

As an illustration the case study of India, a country with 520 million population may be reviewed. India has 2.4 percent of the world's total land area and supports 14 percent of the world's total population. There are 21 million births each year (along with nine million abortions) and eight million deaths, leaving a balance of 13 million people added each year to the already over-populated country. The major cause of this phenomenon is the rapid decline in death rates resulting from the successful health programmes, even though there is still much to be done in this area. The life expectancy has risen from 32 years in 1950 to 51 years in 1968. Health manpower and health facilities are deficient when compared to international standards of developed countries. There is one physician for 5,800 population and 0.5 hospital beds for 1,000 population. Rural health in particular requires attention, and many programmes dealing with communicable diseases and environmental sanitation require funds. Maternal and child health services require augmentation. Health planning has been integrated in the socio-economic development of the country. In spite of three five-year plans the per capita income continues

111

to be below 100 U.S. dollars. The main reason why the Indian economy continues to be an "economy of shortages" is the country's excessive population growth.

The Government of India has declared as its objective to reduce its present birth rate from 41 per thousand to 25 if not 20 per 1,000 as expeditiously as possible. Much credit goes to India's Prime Minister, Mrs. Indira Gandhi and Dr. S. Chandrasekhar, her able Minister in Charge of Family Planning.

Pilot studies in India showed that 66 percent of couples with three children are in favour of family planning. Hence the problem of motivation is not there. Of the 105 million married couples in the country it is estimated that 90 million couples are in the reproductive age group and 80 percent of them are in the rural areas. All the mass media are used to convey the message of family planning and to extol the ideal of small families.

The programme is integrated in the general health services with additional workers to carry out a mass campaign in the urban and rural areas. Besides the conventional contraceptives that are supplied to all that seek, I.U.D. (intra-uterine devices), sterilization of the male and female voluntarily wishing such a procedure after having three children, and oral contraceptives are offered to selected groups. About 4.2 million sterilizations (of which 90 percent were vasectomies) were performed up to June 1968. About 2.4 million I.U.D.s have been inserted so far. Due to the lack of "after care" services this procedure is lagging behind. There are many logistic problems in the programmes but they are being solved. All the family planning services are available at 26,202 centres all over the country, made up of 1,815 urban centres, 5,133 main rural health centres and 19,254 rural sub-centres. Training programmes have been actively taken up. So far 13,087 doctors and 120,520 paramedical personnel have been trained to assist the doctors. Family planning is also included in the curricula of medical students and of nurses. In the last three national plans, family planning has been taken up as a major public health programme. It may be said that this is a mass movement and a mass programme, gaining momentum every day.

There are, however, certain drawbacks, and of them the most important is the low literacy rate, especially amongst the women. Beliefs, faiths, and customs are hard to change. Innovations have yet to be introduced in combinations that would have a sustained momentum. That family planning, nutrition, education and sanitation programmes require a literate basis is shown in a survey of agriculture practices in India. "It was found that the number of improved practices adopted per farmer directly related to levels of educational attainment suggesting that while illiterate peasants may adopt a single simple practice, the wide spread adoption of a combination of new techniques under conditions of illiteracy may prove to be a slow process."

The Government of India is taking suitable action to liberalize "abortion" and also raise the age of marriage for girls to 18 from 15. The education of all married couples in planning their families is also being taken up.

In this great effort, the cooperation of voluntary organizations, the independent medical profession, and the international organizations like the WHO and UNICEF has been a great factor.

There is a need to realize the importance of an ecological approach to the problems of health, and to recognize that each country must select its own *modus operandi*, suitable to its needs, as there is no international blueprint for the development of health services. It has been said by a great social scientist that if you want to plan the world, plan the nation, and if you want to plan the nations, plan the families.

1. — From 1969 World Population Data Sheet prepared by the Population Reference Bureau, 1755 Massachusetts Avenue, N.W., Washington, D.C. (Data quoted by Dr. Rao at the Teach-In were for an earlier period. The editors have chosen instead to give the most recent data.)

2. — *The Cost of Sickness and the Price of Health* (WHO Publication).

3. — See the *Third Report on World Health Situation, 1961-64* (WHO, April, 1967).

4. — See *Second Ten Years of the W.H.O., 1958-1967*, and document A21/P & B/9, April, 1968.

5. — *Report on the World Social Situation, 1965* (UN Publication) p. 88.

ECONOMICS AND POPULATION GROWTH

Colin Grant Clark

Colin Grant Clark is the Director of the Institute for Research in Agricultural Economics and Professorial Fellow of Brasenose College, Oxford. He received post-graduate training at Oxford and Cambridge, worked for some years on economic and social surveys in England and then taught statistics at Cambridge in the 1930's. His first of over a dozen books on economic and social topics was published in 1932. He then spent fourteen years in Australia, first at several universities and later in high-ranking government positions in Queensland. In 1953 he returned to Oxford to his present position. Among his recent publications, are books on "Economics of Irrigation", 1967, and "Population Growth and Land Use", 1967.

Professor Clark is a Roman Catholic active as a laymen at the highest levels of the Church. He was an advisor to Pope Paul VI in the discussions leading to the 1968 Encyclical titled "Humanae Vitae". He is the father of eight children.

World population is now increasing more rapidly than ever before. This is not because parents are having more children, in any country. It is explained entirely by improvements of health and reductions in mortality, which originated in the advanced countries, but are now rapidly spreading all over the world. Experienced micro-biologists tell us that a recrudescence of killing epidemics is possible; but the prospects, on the face of it, are for further large reductions in mortality. In many countries the rate of population increase will accelerate. This would still be the case if all married couples in the world started family planning tomorrow; the increasing number of young people growing up to maturity would ensure further population increase. Africa's population is now 300 million, and the current growth rate of 2.3 percent per year will almost certainly accelerate. China's population (in spite of higher claims sometimes made) is estimated at 650 million, and the maximum rate of growth so far attained has been only a little over one percent per year; but a massive increase in Chinese population will occur in the near future, if order is restored there. Indian population shows an accelerating rate of increase, and may overtake the Chinese in a few decades.

In the nineteenth and twentieth centuries we have seen heavy reductions in the size of family in Europe, North America and Japan. Drastic reductions in the size of families have recently, and very suddenly, appeared in other Asian communities closely linked with our civilization, Taiwan, Hong Kong and Singapore. To infer that family limitation naturally follows increasing wealth is however to over-simplify a complex sociological problem. Recently, an Indian woman doctor was reproaching her servant for having another child. "Why should the *Sirkar* be angry?" asked the servant. Somewhat at a loss for a reason, the doctor replied that the Indian Government was asking its people to limit their families. "Will the Government look after me when I am old?" replied the servant. Parents will not desire to limit their families until (and this limitation still applies to most of the inhabitants of the world) there is an adequately organised system of insurance or social services; and also so long as their children are able to help during the busy seasons on the farm, where every extra pair of hands is needed. This will continue to be the case until there is universal education, and legal prohibition of child labour, which did not come even in Europe until quite late in the nineteenth century.

In advanced societies, where parents cannot put their children to work, but have to provide them with costly upbringing, the desire for family limitation is understandable, and morally legitimate. The moral questions arise over the means employed to obtain it. Family limitation is entirely a question for individual parents. So far as the public welfare is concerned, almost all countries stand to gain, economically and politically, from population increase.

A claim made some years ago by the Food and Agricultural Organization of the United Nations (FAO) that half the world was suffering from malnutrition, has been found to be completely false. After considerable pressure, FAO admitted that they defined as malnourished anyone who did not eat like the inhabitants of Western Europe, many of whom are suffering severely from over-nutrition. Malnutrition has been medically identified among 17 percent of a sample of children in India, and probably exists to a substantial degree in China. In the rest of the world its incidence is limited. Moreover, the means of rapidly increasing food production, anywhere in the world, principally by the application of fertilizers, are ready to hand. The world of the future is much more likely to suffer from an unsaleable glut of farm products, and of people dying from overeating, than food shortage.

If population growth were at the expense of economic progress, we should expect to find the developing countries with the lowest rate of population growth enjoying the highest rates of growth of product per head, and conversely. The facts are found to be to the contrary. A number of economists have shown the factors which cause population growth usually have a beneficial and not adverse effect upon economic growth. By increasing the proportion of young men in the population compared with old, it raises the rate of savings (as has been seen in India). It also reduces per head capital requirements by spreading the cost of large "economic indivisibilities", such as the transport system, over greater numbers. In peasant communities population growth is probably the only force powerful enough to break through the crust of conservatism, and to compel people to adopt more productive agricultural methods. In an industrial country, the advantages of a large and expanding market are clear to every industrialist; and indeed these advantages can be precisely measured.

Until recently, periods of rapid population growth have been rare in the world's history. When these led to pressure on available economic resources, the results have proved to be beneficial, the adoption of more productive methods of agriculture and industry, emigration, cultural and political advance. Examples are the Greeks in the sixth century B.C., the Dutch in the seventeenth century, the English in the eighteenth century, the Japanese in the nineteenth century, and the Indians now. Conversely, French economic historians are blaming the absence of population pressure in early nineteenth century France for their country's comparatively late start in industrialisation.

Whether we like it or not, political influence in the world, and indeed also cultural influence, depends on population. It has been primarily population limitation which has, over the last century, so greatly reduced Western Europe's influence in the world. The powers which will count in the coming decades will be the United States, Soviet Russia, China and India, and perhaps also Pakistan, Japan and Indonesia. The accelerated decline in births now taking place in many Western countries will, in the next generation, greatly reduce our influence in world affairs. It is probably a concealed feeling of racial resentment which causes us to urge so strenuously the Asian, African and Latin American peoples to follow our example.

In addition to the points contained in his previously prepared paper, above, Professor Clark make the following comments.

Professor Dupré had his head so filled with agricultural misinformation that he wanted to rewrite the moral laws to deal with what he believed to be a quite exceptional emergency. The agricultural prospects are much more likely to be a glut of unsaleable agricultural produce. Instead of a world famine I am much more concerned about the people

117

who are going to die as a consequence of overeating. You should see how rapidly the FAO is changing ground all of a sudden. After all they are going to be held responsible if there is an unsaleable glut of wheat and other agricultural products and they have been putting out this misinfor mation about some calorie requirements and half the world being ill-nourished. If you apply the FAO calorie requirement table you reach the conclusion that a large proportion of the population of Japan is living in permanent hunger even though they own television sets and the population of China must have died out several years ago. The most careful calculation one can make of the calorie requirements per head per day in a developing country is somewhere between 1,600 and 2,000. There are quite a number of people who are not getting the required calories, especially in China, but the situation is nothing like that which FAO depicted.

Now, much of the economics I have been listening to is just incredibly naive. A lot of people seem to think that economic growth is something which turns up of its own accord without any serious activity on the part of the population, and therefore they say just let's have fewer population and there will be more all round for all of us. This is not very sensible and it is in conflict with the observed facts.

Let me give you the facts about India. I know India fairly well, having just completed my seventh visit in the last 20 years. The rapid population growth which we now observe only began in the 1930s. Before that India was a country of very slow population growth and for the whole previous century the rate of economic growth in India had been slow. But since population growth in India accelerated we find the rate of economic growth, over the last 20 years, although marred by many defects, has been far faster than India has ever experienced before. Production has increased faster than population at an average gain of 1.5 percent per year. It could have been higher, but even so it is very much higher than the best Indian economists were thinking possible 20 years ago. Everything has improved immensely except agriculture. That is of course very serious as a lot of Indian people are so short of food. Indians I think will be provoked, and very beneficially provoked, by the fact that Pakistan, after a late start, is now making a remarkable success of its agricultural programme, particularly in providing the things which are most needed: more fertilizer, water from wells for irrigation, and roads. Eventually the productivity of Indian agriculture will be improved by better plant genetics, but that is going to take a long time, though there is an enormous room for improvement. The amount of rice which the Indian farmer gets out of each acre of land is just about one-fourth of what the Japanese get. If the Indians understood their agriculture as well as the Japanese understand theirs, the world would be

118

flooded with a deluge of unsaleable rice.

Now turning our attention from India to the developing countries in general, if this remarkably naive economics which I have heard from the other speakers were true, it would unmistakably follow that all the countries with rapid population growth were showing very much worse rates of economic growth per head than the countries with slow population growth. I have taken the figures recently published by the Organization for Economic Cooperation and Development, with headquarters in Paris, which works in close collaboration with the United Nations. It is possible to divide the developing countries into three groups. Those with population growth less than two percent a year, those between two and three percent a year, and those over three percent. Now the countries with the slowest rate of population growth are actually showing a slower rate of growth of product per head, and the higher groups showing about the same rate, about 2.3 percent per head per year, which is a faster rate of growth than that of the United States and Canada. They have now begun to overtake us although it will still be a very slow process. I am not the first economist who has pointed this out. Kuznets, the leading American economist in this field, pointed out that he could detect no effects of population growth in slowing down great economic growth per head. He stated this at the Asian Economic Conference in Delhi but it wasn't what people wanted to hear so they took no notice of it.

These are the facts and you may ask what are the reasons. The economists who have been paying close attention to this problem, although they start out with very different preconceptions from mine, are all coming to the same conclusion that, so far as economics is concerned, the population growth is good and not bad. I refer particularly to the work by Hirschman in Yale, Hagen at the Massachusetts Institute of Technology, and Streeten in Oxford. In the first place a large and growing population gives the industrialist great opportunities for what are known as economies of scale. Every business man knows that you can produce more economically when you are working for a large and growing market than when you are working for a small one. The population growth, far from reducing savings, increases the rate of saving. This was known for some time as a piece of economic theory but it was very interesting to see how it has been confirmed in India, where the rate of saving, which in the early 1950s was only five percent of net national product, rose in recent years to nine percent. There are some exceptions to this rule, as in the case of Sweden. A country like Sweden can form a part of a large world market and be successful in the export trade. At the other end of the scale, there are also some very important exceptions. I refer to small and isolated islands like Barbados and Mauritius. They are so small and so isolated from

119

world trade routes that further agricultural and industrial development is not possible, and in their case the only solution is emigration.

I am asking you to turn your minds right round because you all came here with a preconception that population growth led to poverty, but the problem is really much more interesting. Population growth is much more likely to lead to excessive wealth. Genuine difficulties are going to arise, such as traffic and cars, and too many people using too much water supply, and lack of recreational space. I quite agree with the psychologists when they talk about the importance of man having access to untouched natural beauty in his recreational space. I very heartily agree with what Professor Cole said about the contamination of the atmosphere and of the water. If I had my way I would make myself fearfully unpopular with industrialists and with taxpayers, and with motorists too, in enforcing the very strictest control of pollutants. But do these problems arise from large populations? A country like France with a virtually stationary population has some of the dirtiest rivers in the world. It's their own fault. This is a problem which arises in any wealthy industrial country which has a government which is too feeble to enforce public welfare upon undustrialists.

Now as for Dr. Carstairs' psychiatric fantasy, which was about rats going off their heads, he should talk to historians about this because the days of really dense human settlement, so far as we are concerned, are in the past. Our ancestors did live in desperately overcrowded conditions, but in all the modern cities, and I am referring also to modern cities in Latin America and Asia, they are spreading out. The modern cities on the average are spreading out to an exceptionally low density of only around 10,000 persons per square mile. That's why they take up so much space. However, it is helping to mitigate the traffic problem. The trouble with our cities is not population growth, it is once again our own mismanagement. Let me tell you very briefly what we need to do. If we want the traffic to be manageable we must build urban settlements in units of no more than 100,000 population. The traffic men are quite firm about that. It will be possible to group a few of these near together, but in any case I regard the absolute maximum tolerable limit for any city as a million. Toronto is intolerable by a factor of two or three already. We will have to find some way of breaking up our excessively large cities and dispersing our industrial population over the enormous areas of land which are still at our disposal. And it is only in this way that it will be perfectly easy to give our wealthy motorized population a clean water supply and all the access to open space for recreation which they are likely to need.

Now let me leave you to wallow in your wealth and come back once again to the problems of the hungry countries. Don't take me as

120

understating the seriousness of some of their difficulties. One of the very serious and perfectly concrete figures which emerges from India was the result of a medical survey of school children indicating that 17 percent of them showed severe signs of protein deficiency. The calorie shortage, although it does exist is rare. Protein shortage is more widespread and does very great harm to growing children. What I do want to say is that this can very quickly be put right. The productivity of Indian agriculture is low for a number of reasons, but from what I have seen I have every confidence that this will be put right shortly.

Now, suppose the whole world decides that it wants to eat in the way you and I do. (Probably better for their health if they didn't.) By applying methods used by good modern farmers—I am not talking about anything which is only known in the laboratory—we could produce the food for one person, and also the wood, on slightly over half an acre per person. Let me point out that the amount of the potentially cultivable land in the world which is now being used is about one-third, at most, of that available, and it is mostly cultivated extremely badly. If we take into account all the potential agricultural land in the world, discounting any land which is unduly cold or has low rainfall, allowing for two crops a year in the humid tropics, then the world has the equivalent of nearly 20 billion acres of agricultural land, which means it could support nearly 40 billion people. I should not say "support." It could overfeed them in the way that you and I are overfed at the present time.

Suppose that instead of eating like North Americans the world decided to eat like the Japanese, who after all are very healthy people. The amount of land required to feed a Japanese is about a third of what is required to feed an American. So the number of people the earth could support in that manner is three times as large. And I also only allowed for two crops a year in the hot humid tropics, whereas in fact recently I have seen a dairy farm in India, using fertilizers and water in suitable abundance, where the maximum production of grazing in a cold climate is six tons of dry weight per acre per year. This dairy farm in India was producing what was expected from laboratory tests, which is to say precisely five times as much as can be produced from temperate land. So if you take that into account, instead of 20 billion acres of land available in the world you would have to put it up to the equivalent of 27 billion and you can overfeed two people per acre or you can feed Japanese style about six people per acre.

So the number of people the world can support is an almost incredibly large figure and I would like to just reassure Dr. Cole that in the course of improving our agriculture in this way we will increase the input of oxygen into the atmosphere as well.

I might indeed give you a small bit of science fiction to finish this subject. I said science fiction, but it is already quite a serious practical problem for the international committee which is designing a project for lunar horticulture. When the first moon settlement occurs—it is probably not many months away now—it has been estimated that transport to the moon settlement will cost 10 million dollars per gram, and so anything moon settlers can do to provide themselves with vegetables will be much appreciated. The best laboratory methods now known show that you can get a rate of photosynthesis of 45 grams dry weight per square metre per day and on this basis, if there were a permanent lunar settlement, the minimum food and fibre for one man could be provided by the continuous cultivation of no more than 27 square metres. So much for science fiction.

I would like to mention a few points in conclusion. The Pope's Encyclical—I was one of the members of his consultative committee—did not condemn family limitation. It is entirely concerned with the moral question of what are permissible and impermissible methods of achieving it. The Pope pointed out that under certain circumstances family limitation may be necessary.

I will have to say one or two things about the problems of morals in religion because the previous Church spokesmen haven't had much to say about it, although I am very grateful to Professor Stycos, who did give us a good deal of religious information. There may be some people here who are completely godless. I think that represents a certain defect in their intelligence. But what is very much worse—I am quoting from a leaflet that was handed out—is when you get people writing that to limit births has placed man in the position of playing God. This is quoted from the Population Reference Bureau who are a bunch of nonentities, but all the same this is actual blasphemy, the sin of pride when Satan set himself up as higher than God. A sense of one's own inferiority to God is a necessary condition to all religion; and sin or immoral conduct is the deliberate faulting of one of God's purposes. Let me make this clear by one or two illustrations.

God taught us how to make all the material wealth which the world possesses, and we are offending against the moral law when we help ourselves to other peoples' goods, or when we acquire goods by means of injustice. We were given the power of speech which animals don't possess, and God's purpose in that was that we should be able to convey true information to each other. And so we are performing an immoral act when we use the power of speech in order deliberately to convey false information.

In the case of sex, God gave us tremendous desire and enjoyment of sex, particularly for males, for the purpose of carrying on the human race.

Now, let me put it to you as an abstract question. Suppose there were no enjoyment in sex, how many conceptions would take place at all? The world wouldn't go on, and this brings us back to what was God's purpose in creating sexual enjoyment—and God did create it. There are some modern theologians who are trying to separate this, and talk about how you can separate the sexual function of marriage from the reproductive function of marriage, but I can't see where they are logically going to stop. Before long they will be condoning divorce and adultery and sodomy.

We are now going through the final stages of the religious year. We have been through the season of Christmas when we were amazed at God's humility in coming down to earth as man. We have been through Good Friday when we grieved that God had to suffer death because of the faults which you and I have committed. We have been through Easter when we rejoiced that God has shown us that death can be overcome. Today, October 27, we are celebrating the feast of Christ the King, and this is Christ giving us commandments, telling us that those who disobey, every one of us, will have to come face to face with Christ at some time in the near or distant future and explain whether we have carried out his commandments or not. And he has promised terrible things for those who persist in disobeying him—much more terrible than any man could have thought of.

THE HUNGER GAP

Georg Borgstrom

Georg Borgstrom was born in Sweden in 1912. He studied at the University of Lund and was awarded the D.Sc. in plant physiology.

Dr. Borgstrom was a member of the faculty at the University of Lund for some years and then became involved in organizing and administering a number of research institutes concerned with food preservation in Sweden. In 1956 he transferred to Michigan State University where he now holds a joint appointment in the departments of food science and geography.

Professor Borgstrom is a member of many scientific societies and academies in a number of countries. He has attended more than 40 important international conferences on food technology, nutrition, biochemistry, etc. His list of publications includes many scientific and technical papers as well as many others that are semi-popular. One of his books "Food for Billions" published in Swedish in 1961, has been translated into a number of other languages. Others include: "Limitations of Man's Existence", 1964; "The Hungry Planet", in 1965; and "Revolution in World Fisheries" in 1966.

After Dr. Clark's excursions into the higher theological spheres, and his joyful wanderings in the world of fairy tales, I would like to take you back to the stark reality of our days—the hunger gap. The gap between 1,100 million people who are reasonably adequately fed, as against 2,400 million who are short of all the basic necessities of life, but primarily food and water. This tremendous gap comes after 20 years of exceptional measures in the post-war period to provide for growing numbers of the human race. Five years ago we realized the tremendous success of modern agriculture and modern fisheries when the FAO made its annual summary of our accomplishments. Nevertheless the true fact was that the world never contained so many undernourished, hungry, thirsty, people as at that stage. We have lost the game due to our fallacious thinking and our inability to see reality.

Constantly I get invitations to scientific meetings about the protein issue of our world. The protein meetings are held, but it is frightening to see the discrepancy between talk and action. We go to conferences, we hide in our research laboratories, we go to debates of this kind, and forget the enormous urgency. We have only ten years to act if we are going to regain control of man's destiny.

We will be faced with 1,000 million more people to take care of in the next ten years. No economist, food scientist, politician, nor any expert in any field, has really addressed himself to this very critical issue. And at the same time, we need to double the world's present agricultural production to provide for those that are now living. The hungry have not the slightest interest in what Professor Colin Clark may think or what I may elaborate to you. They are interested in one thing: what can be done to alleviate their situation. I humbly submit that there is not the slightest truth behind all these, in my opinion, disgraceful calculations showing that the world could feed many billions, calculated on the basis of areas per head with the assumptions about fertilizer, about water, about soil, etc., etc. It is a terrible scandal that the world is not now taking care of more than one billion out of three and one half billion.

Let us for a moment analyse the hunger gap. You know the traditional analysis, the backwardness of these other people, their flickering creativity, their notorious listlessness. They say our success is due to our impressive creativity, our famous ingenuity, our resourcefulness, and, not the least, our technical superiority. Do these white apologists not know that peoples of this other world, which is now on the other side of the hunger gap, had created and developed all the advances in civilization in ages prior to ours?

Some impugn religion in this analysis, saying that they have a negative attitude to life. Look at the fatalism of the Mohammedan, the ascetism of the Hindu, the contemplation of the Buddhists; all these create a negative, passive attitude. As Christians, we have a positive attitude. I am particularly amused at this argument because in America I discover hints in the press that we Protestants—I happen to be Protestant—are the ones that are to be credited with the exceptional technical development of the United States. The Catholics are represented as having a negative non-progressive attitude. A false, equally naive analysis.

There are much more fundamental reasons. Some of the world's poor are supposed to work a whole week on what we would consider one day's food supply. You try that and you will get deathly tired. But this is not the most ominous aspect. In the critical growing ages of childhood, shortage of protein causes brain damage which induces mental backwardness. If the protein needed to build up the brain tissue and the nerve tissue is in short supply when these tissues are growing, then they do not develop properly and no diet later in life will change this.

The most important aspect of our apparent superiority relates to historical factors. There was never in history a group of men that conquered a greater storehouse of protein than the white men that came to break the prairies in Canada and the United States. These are the richest agricultural lands of the globe. We killed and chased away as many Indians as we could. The white man also took the remaining part of the hemisphere, and did the same with the Indians there, and got in return the second most important agricultural region in the world, the pampas of Argentina. We got such enormous riches that we didn't have sufficient manpower to exploit them. So we went hunting and trading for manpower, creating the most disgraceful ages in our history. Fourteen to 20 million African people were imported to this continent. The number involved was really twice that because there was "wastage," those who were killed or died in the hunt, at the dispatching ports, at the receiving ports.

We took up positions in Africa, on the highlands, and took the best lands that were available there. We made India British, the East Indies Dutch; we went to Asia and took a great number of power positions there for purposes of trade. It was all organized to provide for the white man. This explains why we today possess far greater resources—twice, three times, up to 20 times more land than any of these other countries. We are rich because or ancestors were rapacious.

Well, you may say, this is not now true of Europe, particularly some of the Western European countries. They are still depending on enormous resources of land in other countries to feed themselves. There still is a constant flow. They still own a great deal of land and property and determine to what use it is going to be put. I don't think that the world can continue to allow one-third of the world's population to use two-thirds of the world's agricultural and fishery resources. We need a more equitable distribution. We need a new pattern for world trade to bring this really into focus.

The world fisheries industry has passed through one of its most successful periods in its entire history, with an enormous mobilization of the oceans, led by the Soviet Union and Japan. This tremendous use of the resources has resulted in a doubling of the world's catch since 1953. And we talk about this as an immense contribution to the hungry of the world. But only a few pitiful percent go the hungry. Over 50 percent of these growing catches of the ocean goes to feed our broilers, our hogs. A great fish meal industry was created in Peru in less than five years, which was a most remarkable accomplishment; almost its entire production is used to feed poultry in the Western World—two-thirds goes to Europe, one-third goes to the United States.

To have the hungry feeding the well-satisfied is absurd. The most important initiative, in my opinion, that the United Nations ever took was to initiate the so-called United Nations Conferences of Trade and Development. The first one was held in Geneva in 1964 which was a clear effort to get re-adjustment in this uneven, inequitable distribution of all the world's riches. What happened? Each group, the hungry on the one hand and the well-fed on the other, made their proclamations and pronouncements, presented their studies and suggestions, but there was no meaningful effort to coordinate this. At Geneva the rich world promised to put at the disposal of the hungry world one percent of our gross national products. Once again a pittance, but we failed. Only one country of the old world managed to reach this extremely low figure.

The pittance would not pay more than a fraction of the losses the hungry world has encountered due to developments since 1952: the price and value of their raw products exported to us have been going down, and down, and down, while the value of the capital goods and industrial products these people were supposed to be buying according to our nineteenth-century concepts were going up, and up, and up.

In New Delhi we were a little more careful. The rich world no longer promised to give one percent. We promised to try to give one percent. But a demand for justice is taking the place of begging for charity. We have long ago passed the point where charitable deliveries were sufficient.

I agree that we cannot carry calories successfully round the world, although we have been doing it for our benefit for several hundred years and are still doing it. But this is basically the wrong approach. Protein will always be needed in tremendous quantity because, besides calories, it is necessary in nutrition. I think FAO is on firm ground with their figures, in fact those figures appear to be on the low side judging from the findings that nutritional experts have made in studies on all the continents. These experts have demanded that the figures be adjusted upwards rather than downwards. Yet we still have people saying that their calorie needs are smaller than ours, they are lower in stature, they weigh less, they eat less, and they don't need as much as we. A study in Africa recently showed that 20 percent of all calories have to be used to get water. And water is our planet's most critical issue. We in America are going to go crazy before we go thirsty, and we are going to get thirsty before we go hungry. This is our sequence, but it is not the sequence of this other world.

If we could use every drop of available water effectively in production we could provide for 20-25 billion people. But everyone realizes that this is one of those theoretical exercises. We can never expect to use more than one-fourth of this water. A lot of it is falling on desert and on other land areas where it immediately evaporates. The fact is that if all people were to live on the American standard we couldn't provide for more than 500 million people.

It has been said that only one-third of the globe is used for agriculture; it has even been said that only one-tenth is used. Of what is available, 27 percent is used as pastures, very little of which could be ploughed and farmed more intensively to our long-run advantage. It is unanimously agreed that pastures are relatively poor lands, poorer than those which are now in cultivation, which is reasonable on the assumption that man hasn't been a complete fool. We are cultivating today 10.7 percent. I think that all analyses agree that it is not feasible, on the basis of any kind of calculation, to cultivate over 30 percent. It would of course mean further reduction of the forest acreages, and of the pastoral acreages.

This is the century of irrigation. We have doubled the world's irrigated acreage since the beginning of the century. India and China, which we like to call underdeveloped, have led the world in this intensive technical development. Started 5,000 years ago, many of their irrigation works are still in operation. We have put immense effort into irrigating more land and have doubled it, which is a majestic accomplishment. We will get a second doubling before the end of the century with those big dams which are now being built and all the wells that are being drilled. When we have done that the remaining water would be about sufficient to irrigate less than half of the Sahara and provide adequate food for less than 200 million people. Clearly the agricultural resources for producing food are and will remain very limited in terms of the potential future size of the human population.

I have not mentioned the most ominous feature of the hunger gap. That is the fact that this other world is growing twice as fast as we are growing. Not due to any miraculous increase in birth rate, but due to reduced infant mortality. We have today a dismal picture, far more serious than our figures show, which I have seen in my travels around all corners of this globe. No one is speaking on behalf of the exploited and suffering children of the world. We supposedly have a UNICEF organization in the United Nations. Do you realize that they never reach more than one-tenth of the children of the world? The children in many countries are not registered until after the third year. Over half of them die before the age of five and they are not in any of our figures.

We see millions of people being dumped into cities through the excessive pressure on the countryside. We insist in talking of farms in this world where there are really only plots. One to two acres is the common size of the farm, often subdivided into five, and I have even seen twelve subdivisions of such small plots. It is in India, China, Japan, Indonesia, and in parts of Latin-America that people are forced to eke out their existence on small plots like this. We now like to think that industry is attracting them to the cities. In some cases this is true, but the major driving force is the extreme over-pressure on the countryside.

The cities of the immediate future will not be pitiably small like Tokyo or New York, but will be aggregations of 20, 30, 40, 50 million people. There is no food scientist, no architect, nor anyone else that has addressed himself to how these people are going to be accommodated. We already have squatter cities, cities of 100,000 in Latin America, where 70 percent of the people live under these obnoxious conditions. In the bigger cities one-third live under these conditions. Look at Kenya, growing today at three percent per year, while the cities are growing twice as fast at six percent per year. What does this do to alleviate conditions in the countryside? Almost nothing. The increase in the cities of Kenya will have to be 38 percent if they are going to take care of what is now the increase in the countryside.

Still we insist on our old models. It is high time that we got new models in place of the kind of miraculous economic thinking behind the idea that excessive populations are producing affluence. If this were the truth, why on earth are China and India, these extremely impoverished countries, not at the very peak of affluence. Population growth is being confused with economic development. There may be an early stage where a relationship could be possible, but to say that this is in the future is to be ridiculous. We have the spectacle of Argentina putting out one book after the other about the day when they are going to be a grand power with 100 million people. And so is Brazil and so is Mexico. And even some Canadians seem to hold to this view.

There are many more fallacies that we could examine but we had better let the stark realities of life come to the foreground and be the basis of our discussion. And remember that the older generation to which I belong has failed miserably in taking care of the world's affairs. We have managed to start two world wars and we are doing our best to get a third started. I think what the world needs are two billion angry men and women fired by holy wrath, making it clear to their governments and their leaders that this earth should not become the scene of a grand demise, man's annihilation. These two billion should demand, in accordance with the Atlantic Charter, that the world's resources be utilized for the common benefit of mankind. We could begin in the ocean. We have to make ends meet, and I agree that we are the last generation that has this chance to save humanity. It will certainly not be possible to crowd the equivalent of the present world population into Ontario, as a "young editor" in a local Toronto newspaper has recently suggested. I have seen similar calculations crowding the whole population into Michigan, into the British Isles, into some Baltic islands, as if the future were to live in prison, or in cemeteries, or in rabbit hutches.

Exploding humanity is a frightful crisis. Don't resort to the fairytales of futurology, promising pie in the sky or a golden future, with limitless abundance and excess leisure, a life of bliss. We should instead be aware that if we do not want to change anything, everything will change.

Tomorrow's agenda should have been yesterday's. Which are the crucial points on this agenda? First, a recognition of the interwoven destinies of the entire mankind. The Golden Rule, basic to all religions, has become identical to supreme statesmanship and prudent action. The world is inescapably *One*. This is far more than a cliché. Second, a realization of the self-evident fact that the globe is finite and man, despite all technology, fatefully dependent on its limitations. Humble respect for the laws of living nature and a sense of responsibility as guardians of the earth's riches are irrevocable imperatives. The third point on man's agenda is the urgent mobilization of all resources of the globe in a superhuman effort to regain control of man's destiny—this requires a General Staff of Peace, nationally and internationally, as well as a drastic switch in man's priorities. Fourth and finally and not the least essential, a new education that is truly universal.

DISCUSSION FOLLOWING THIRD SESSION

Mr. Cadbury:

First of all let us give the opportunity to anyone on the platform who may wish to raise any questions.

Dr. Stycos:

I would prefer to make a comment. Dr. Clark is quite correct I think in pointing out some of the deficiencies in our information about the relationship between economic development and population growth, and indeed it is the case that statistics can be marshalled to show an absence of relationship very often between these two. This is merely to demonstrate that population growth is not the only determinant of economic growth. There are very few people today I think that would maintain that population growth by itself can either produce or prevent economic growth.

Suppose you were travelling in an underdeveloped country and had occasion to meet a high official in the field of education. If you asked him if it would make any difference to him if, in the next five years, there were half as many births or half as many students entering schools, given his very low allocation of resources for improving education, what do you expect his answer would be? Here would be a kind of practical test to see what policy makers think of the relation between economic development and population growth.

But lest I be accused of more economic naivety let me pass to greener pastures in sociology where I may turn the tables on Dr. Clark. Rarely in this year of 1968 have I heard more old sociological chestnuts pulled out than in the case of Dr. Clark's talk. His attribution to the Indian woman of a desire to have large families is the kind of thing which we heard in the 1950's. But in the past ten years Indian social scientists have been valiantly and I think correctly doing some of the most important and impressive pieces of research on attitudes that have ever been done on a single subject before. If there is one thing that is clear it is that the Indian woman is not so foolish as to want ten starving children to support her in her old age, nor is the Indian man so foolish as to wish five sons in order to farm a piece of land the size of postage stamp. This kind of attribution of attitudes to lower classes in the population is entirely characteristic of a period in which we had no empirical information on the subject.

If we want *evidence* in the world of behaviour, rather than non-expert opinions, I would ask you to look at the case of Latin America where induced abortions in the cities are becoming an extreme problem. In most of the cities of Latin America abortion is performed by means of a long and sharp instrument. The net result of this is pain, danger, cost. The woman who has an abortion incurs not only these but also may be accused of having performed an illegal act and a sinful act. In spite of this we note that last year in Santiago, Chile's capital city, one out of every three blood transfusions in the hospital wards of the obstetrical service of the city of Santiago went to a woman haemorrhaging from an abortion. In other words I think if we do not provide modern methods women will adopt the age-old methods. Women have been kept in the thirteenth century too long, it is time they were rescued.

Dr. Rao:

I would like to make a point regarding the economics of health. Take the analogy of India where there are 21 million births and nine million abortions annually, of which we don't know how many are induced, endangering the mother's life and also her health. We find that four million children die below the age of 14. What an economic waste it is. We find about 50 percent of these total deaths in India in children, about 10 percent of whom die under the age of one. The money value of man has been worked out in U.S. rates and comparable figures can be assigned to other countries. To bring up a baby costs about 3,000 dollars, to bring it up to the age of three costs about 6,000 dollars, and by the age of 12 it costs 16,000 to 18,000 dollars. Well all this is an investment and if you are going to lose children below the age of 14 you can see how much it is an economic case. Why is it that these children are dying? They are dying of communicable diseases, and it is malnutrition that is killing them with these diseases. If we want to prevent these deaths then naturally we have got to adopt a means so that they can have food. Without food you cannot build up a nation. And naturally to prevent these deaths from abortions, from child death, from other factors, it is necessary to have planned parenthood and necessary to give spacing of children. We believe the mother is the key to the happiness of the family. And unless the mother is given the freedom to have a child when she likes or to determine the number of children there can be no happiness for the peoples of the world.

Mr. Cadbury:

Dr. Clark's theory that to be powerful people must be numerous is

134

rather startling. Indonesia is about the sixth largest country in the world. It's rather a long way from power. I would like to ask him what his definition of power is. Perhaps power may be interpreted more realistically as influence. There are a lot of small countries with small groups of people with great influence. But I would like to ask him to elaborate on this a little because I find this a very difficult thesis to understand.

Dr. Clark:
    I think before long Indonesia will be a powerful country.

Mrs. Alice Cowan:
    I would like to read a poem and then ask a question.
        Please, yes, not done,
        Please, yes, not done,
        Too many other things to do,
        But suffering can wait for
        Marches of protest,
        Marches of refined aggression,
        Coffee with the girls,
        Demands from uncle,
        The late, late show.

        The world grows, its faces shrink,
        Babies get born, mothers laugh and wink,
        Not enough food for every mouth,
        Not enough love for every heart,
        Not enough affection for every soul,
        Please, yes, not done,
        Please, yes, not done.
    Dr. Stycos, you said that North American efforts in the area of population control were impotent because of Latin-American suspicion of the United States. Surely we in Canada can't be lumped together with the United States. Can you give us some suggestions as to what *our* nation and *we* as individuals *can* do?

Dr. Stycos:
    Rather than say what Canada should do, let me say what I think the effect would be if it chose to do something. Canada, like the United States, is very highly respected in Latin America but, unlike the United States, is not feared. This very important distinction, which relates to almost anything Canada could do in Latin America, holds particularly true in the possible area of technical and financial assistance in population

135

programming. Canada is viewed more like a rich cousin than like a millionaire-general. There is fear that the United States is looking for new lands and new resources for its people in Latin America, or is attempting to exploit Latins to hold them down; it would be very unlikely that these kinds of motivations would be attributed to Canadians. I think that the evidence of success of the Swedish program in Latin America is good evidence that the Latins are looking for alternatives to United States assistance in this area.

The only other piece of cautious and contingent advice which I would dare to give Canadians is this: if you are planning to go into the area of international technical assistance in the field of family planning by all means put your own house in order first.

Mr. Cadbury:

I can't resist the temptation to say that there is plenty Canadians can do. What is needed is the mobilization of the opinion to do those things, and we can obviously join in that mobilization. First of all let us get our own law in order, because that will release the second possibility which is to get Canadians active and the Canadian government active in this field, and to help other countries in the way they want to be helped. That is not happening because of our domestic law and it is insufficiently understood by our legislators how important it is that the law be changed and the external aid department of our government be released to be active.

Questioner:

Dr. Clark, I have the impression that you feel certain kinds of birth control are not right because they either produce immorality among the people or because they act against the will of God or something like this. I feel that it is immoral to bring children into the world that can't be fed, clothed, or given an education. How can you say that it is right to bring ten or 12 children into the world when parents can perhaps only support two or three in a meagre way?

Dr. Clark:

The answer is that if the family is really starving they should not produce more children but you mustn't assume that all families are starving.

Questioner:

But it was pointed out that two-thirds of the people in the world are under-nourished.

Dr. Clark:

They are not. That is an incorrect statement.

Questioner:

Dr. Clark, am I to understand from the manner in which you universally involved us all in a classification of time into Christian seasons that you imply as a solution to world economic imbalance and population problems that everyone convert to Christianity or Catholicism, and further that if this is not done then that no other solution is worth trying?

Dr. Clark:

I didn't say that nor did I intend to say that.

Questioner:

Dr. Clark, people use pills every day for many reasons to help control their body chemistry for their own good, and I was wondering why then is it considered unholy or sinful to use contraceptive pills which were developed to help control man's body chemistry for his own good.

Dr. Clark:

If you are genuinely treating an illness or abnormality they are morally permissible, but if you are using them to prevent normal consequences of coition they are not.

Questioner:

Dr. Clark came here to discuss population and his answer to the population problem was that there wasn't any such problem. But there is a stark imbalance in the distribution of wealth, and this is an in-built feature of the market system and the power-politic system in effect at the present date. Can Dr. Clark see any bloodless way of redistributing this wealth to produce a reasonable degree of equity in the world?

Dr. Clark:

There is a very marked imbalance in the distribution of wealth and it is in the poorest countries that the distribution is most unequal. I think the evidence is that the operation of the free-market system is likely to put it right whereas the operation of communism is likely to rigidify distribution as it has in Russia.

Questioner:

I would like to ask panel members what they think about the ethics, the possibilities of implementation, and also the effectiveness of eugenics. I would like to make the point as a geneticist that there is trouble in marriage guidance counselling in this respect. People are heterozygous in some factor which would, say, produce a disease in some of their children if they married and bore children. If such a person is advised not to marry another who is also heterozygous, then this factor remains in the population. The factor will spread producing a mounting problem generation by generation.

Dr. Rao:

There may be medical reasons, social reasons, or economic reasons for the limitation of a pregnancy. As far as medical reasons are concerned, individual illnesses such as kidney, heart, or pulmonary diseases may prohibit normal completion of a pregnancy. Also there are disorders which are genetically transmitted from parent to child; once these are diagnosed permanent measures of sterilization may be advisable. In fact, contraceptive measures are absolutely necessary in cases of congenital disorders.

Questioner:

Dr. Clark advanced the thesis that population growth is desirable because it leads to greater efficiency in the production and distribution of goods, and therefore results in an increase in our standard of living. However, Lamont Cole has pointed to our unwillingness to pay the cost of waste disposal, and this is doing serious damage to our economy. Also, if we practice more intensive agriculture, what about the possibility of serious agricultural pests expanding and overwhelming our efforts?

Dr. Clark:

I heartily agree with what Dr. Cole says and I think the pollution which he described can be cured if we are willing to make the effort and pay the expense. As agricultural production increases we will face new pests but I am optimistic about the ability of scientists to meet them.

Questioner:

Dr. Clark, you give as a solution to the problem in Barbados that there should be emigration. But Canada, United States and England, which are the only places that can really help in this problem, have very limited quotas. I would like another solution to solve the problem there.

Dr. Clark:

The question is quite unanswerable. The conduct of all the three countries has been indefensible.

Questioner:

Dr. Clark, since you don't think there is any need for population growth control now, don't you think that when this need arises, since the world is only so big, that the problem will be much harder to deal with because there will be so many more people to contend with?

Dr. Clark:
I think that's a long way away in the future.

Summary of Discussion by the Radio Panel.

Mr. McKee:
Dr. Keenleyside, may we have your comments on Dr. Clark's speech?

Dr. Keenleyside:
It would be quite impossible to deal in detail with all the matters that Dr. Clark discussed in his address. I have known Dr. Clark for the last 25 years. I have discussed his problems and his view of them with him. I have also heard the discussions of other professional economists in relation to Dr. Clark's views. He has steadily become more extreme in his statement of the unimportance of the population problem and as his views have become more extreme those of his critics have become more divergent from his own. In fact I know of no other economist of any standing in the world who supports Dr. Clark, particularly when he goes to the point of saying, as he did this afternoon, that there will be no real problem in providing food for 40 billion people. Now even if it were possible to accept this statement, the idea of having 40 billion people in the world is so abhorrent that I find it very difficult to justify his complaisance in relation to the whole problem of population growth. If we had 40 billion people we would be living in a sort of hen-house battery arrangement which would belie all the things which we have been saying about the value of our life. The whole quality of human life is the thing that we have been discussing in the Teach-In, and it is essential to do something about the population growth to ensure that the quality of life can be improved.
Dr. Clark is the only really outstanding economist in the world who adopts the old position of the Catholic Church before the modern trend occurred in it. He was known all over the world as a man who went perhaps even farther than the papacy in saying that there was no problem here and it would be unnecessary to do anything about it. I think it was probably wise of the Pope to put him on the committee because if he had been left off the papacy would have been accused of having forgotten to take into account the views of the strongest proponent of the old attitude towards this problem.

139

Mr. McKee:

How do you relate the statements made by Dr. Clark today to the Canadian situation?

Dr. Keenleyside:

I think Dr. Clark was wrong in suggesting as he did, by inference at least, that we had unlimited arable land in this country that would enable us to maintain here a very enormous population. The fact of the matter is that most soil experts will tell us that the amount of land that is usable in Canada is very much more limited than one would imagine from looking at the map. The greater part of the really useful soil of our country is already being employed, but that is not to say that we could not maintain more people on the land and certainly we could maintain many more people on the lands of Canada if we are prepared to maintain them at about the level of existence that pertains in contemporary China.

FOURTH SESSION

A DILEMMA FOR AFFLUENTS

ECOLOGY AND DISCRETION

Ian McTaggart Cowan

Ian McTaggart Cowan was born in Edinburgh, Scotland in 1910, and was transplanted to Vancouver, Canada at the age of three. He studied biology at the University of British Columbia and then ecology at the University of California at Berkeley where he received his Ph.D.

Dr. McTaggart Cowan joined the faculty of the University of British Columbia in 1940 and has remained there since, holding a number of academic posts. He is now Professor of Zoology and Dean of the Faculty of Graduate Studies.

His research interests have centered on the evolution and ecology of mammals and birds and have led to the publication of some 150 papers and two books. He has been a leader in applying ecological knowledge to the management of biological resources. He has participated in various national and regional surveys and commission on parks, game and fish. His social concern for the integrity of the natural environment has been expressed in hundreds of public lectures, and in various executive positions with national and international conservation bodies including the International Union for the Conservation of Nature.

Professor McTaggart Cowan has helped frame Canadian ecological research policies through membership on the National Research Council the Fisheries Research Board of Canada and various professional organizations. He designed and produced several educational television shows that have won international awards.

The world of today may be roughly divided into two groups each with many millions of people. The members of one group are now as in the remote past concerned with the day-to-day struggle to stay alive. But for the members of the second group the preoccupation with survival is several generations behind, and their concern is not with survival but with the quality of living.

The "survival" people find themselves either steadily or periodically in circumstances where food, clothing, and shelter for themselves and their families cannot be obtained with the resources they can muster. For many of them the matter of discretionary use of resources for what we might say are "non-essentials" to survival is no part of their experience or of their hope.

The dramatic differences between the two is basically the result of the discovery and development of the thought processes of science and the flow of science-based competence into an elaborate technology. The countries whose people have participated vigorously in the scientific revolution have been able to alter the opportunities open to their people in almost every sector of human experience. Most important of all, however, has been the successful assault upon the vital questions, the matter of who dies, when and of what. The biomedical sciences have succeeded in interfering dramatically with the birth rate which was evolved to surmount a primitive death rate. As a result the average human life span has almost doubled, and the comfort and well-being with which man in the developed countries traverses his life has greatly increased.

The harnessing of physical and biological energy to man's purposes has created situations in which the resources available to the individual greatly exceed the basic needs, and so has provided a surplus above biological necessities to be devoted to discretionary uses. Thus one of the most important differences between the technological cultures and the folk cultures is the extent of discretionary use of resources and the nature of the impact this has upon the soil, water, air, and biota of the world in which man lives, and, going full cycle, on the future of man himself.

While one can point to science-based technology as the source of these differences, the inventions arising from this source have demanded rapid change in social ingenuity. The altered death rate has meant many more people and has created challenges that have found their responses in more efficient food production, food processing and storage, transportation and communication and more effective "insulation" of man from the rigours of his natural environment. The adoption of these and the multitude of other processes and devices invented by technological man have only been possible by virtue of concomitant social innovation and major changes in patterns of trade, government, conscience, and expectations.

Periods of particularly rapid evolution almost inevitably result in uneven rates of change in the different components. Probably the most pervasive fact of the last century is the crescendo of change in the physical competence at our disposal. It has been suggested by many that this has, in many sectors, outstripped our capacity to respond socially and has thus led to the distress and discontent so prevalent today even in the most positive societies.

At the same time we have been very varied in the manner in which we have exported these advantages of our invention. We exported first whaling, religion, Victorian morality with its burden of shame, economics, and death control. And this has had profound influence on the peoples to

142

which we exported them. The life-lengthening inventions have been most acceptable and have readily entered all the folk cultures to which we have brought them. However, human fecundity and the behaviour toward it had evolved through all human history to overwhelm the primitive mortality factors. Interference with the death rate left the equation unbalanced and the population explosion was inevitable. In many areas one can truly say that the outcome has been the exchange of one sort of misery for another

I would like to read a very brief quotation from the first volume of *The World Food Problem* published in 1967 by a very distinguished group of scholars that examined this problem for the President of the United States. My quotation is: "the stark misery of hunger, the ravages of malnutrition, the threats of civil strife, social unrest, and political upheaval posed by food shortages and the shadow cast by impending famine have all been portrayed in urgent and compelling terms." I am not going to enter the argument as to whether there is a population explosion or whether there is a shortage of food. There are millions that will die this year that are going to settle that argument.

Never before have we been more rapidly and more vividly aware in our part of the world of the tragedies and unhappiness that afflict so many people. Furthermore, we are no longer willing to accept these misfortunes as the visitations of angry gods, as the workings of an inscrutable providence or as the consequence of our disobeying some supposed divine law. The integrated systems view of the world, which is the life blood of the scientific approach to problem solving, has convinced us all that problems have causes and are solvable given sufficiently rigorous attack. And many of us now are asking: How do we in our rich society devote our technological competence, our social experience, our educational effectiveness and some of our wealth to helping those less fortunate nations raise their own standards of living in their own particular manner?

At the same time no one of even the wealthiest nations has cause to be satisfied with the state of all its citizens, nor with its impact on the environment from which it draws its well-being and the quality of the life its people can live now and in the future.

My part in this series of discussions is to focus our thoughts for a few minutes upon some of the most important targets for Canadian internal policy in this context in the years ahead. As an ecologist my primary concern is with the consequences of the size of our population in Canada and the results of our economic and political attitudes and practices upon the living resources and environments of this country of ours. The intimate relationships that exist between the state of the environment and the quality of our lives and what this means in our capacity to help others inevitably introduces strong social connotations.

143

Our effectiveness in identifying the issues and in designing our national and personal behaviour toward them appropriately will not only influence the kinds of lives Canadians can live but will also materially influence our ability to aid others. If we fail to comprehend the desperate path down which all of us in this world are now rushing, or if we fail to act effectively toward the events of today and of the foreseeable future, not only will we be damaging our own well-being, but also restricting our capacity to help elsewhere.

It is most difficult to think about policy without a reasonable image of what our goals are and this is precisely what we lack today. We are busy building a world in which ever more of our pleasures have to be taken in consuming things, rather than enjoying quiet, the beauty of nature or reflective or creative tasks in which we can all find genuine interest and fulfilment.

On all sides we are now beginning to hear the harsh voices of dissent, but you have to listen hard for the cadence of a better tomorrow because it is almost inaudible.

Then we—too and I speak of my generation—are thinking and planning for people still very young. They cannot escape being different from us—but how different and in what ways. What kind of society will they find most pleasing? Will they still be hog-tied by our cult of the quantitative in which it is assumed that if it is more abundant it is better, and it doesn't matter whether it is the traffic-stopping vital statistics of some unfortunate girl on Wall Street, or whether it is the increasing population of Inuvik, or the number of indestructible beer cans that we have strewed on the surface of our contaminated countryside—if it is bigger it must be better. Will profitability still be the primary basis of morality in the world that most of you here are thinking and planning for? I hope it won't.

It seems basic that we should be aiming for a more satisfying life for every participant in Canada's future as well as for the creation of circumstances that will permit our country to meet its external destiny.

As Taylor, in The Biological Time Bomb has so well said: "The root of our problem, pragmatically, is the absence of any means of measuring satisfaction, and our tendency to assume that an economically calculated standard of living is actually a measure of satisfaction. When we read that the output of goods reached a new peak, we usually assume this made people happier. But if it was achieved by sacrificing conditions of life which they greatly value, it may have made them, on the balance, less happy. And by conditions I don't mean merely extrinsic conditions, like privacy in an unpolluted atmosphere, but also intrinsic conditions like the intensified level of anxiety, a frustrated emotional life, or an increase in crime."

144

I am going to start with three premises. You can accept them or deny them, but I will give you them. First, that our population in Canada is going to increase for some time ahead. Second, that the majority of the increase will cluster in ever larger and more crowded cities. Finally, I can see little reason to doubt that for the short term at least the patterns of social development on this continent will demand of each of us an ever smaller portion of our lives for earning a living. It is axiomatic to me that there will be more time in which to cultivate those activities of life that make us distinctively human. We will be able to devote more of our resources to activities of choice—I used the word discretion in my title—and if we wish it, more time for socially important endeavours to the assistance of those of our less fortunate colleagues in the world today.

I have not found any convincing arguments that more people here or elsewhere will result in a general improvement in our way of life. I do not find any good reason for espousing the Chamber of Commerce attitude that more consumers leads inevitably to greater happiness for all in an ever improving environment for man. To the contrary we see on every side evidence of dislocation within our social evolution and massive alteration of ecological processes in the environment to the point where they are already harmful to our present and future well-being.

I am confident that we could correct the errors in our own society and build a nation in which for some years we could tolerate our present rate of increase, which is not a very rapid one, and build a healthy, happy, satisfying life for our citizens, but if this is to be there must be some deep-seated changes in our social and in our ecological attitudes. On the other hand we must now recognize that the world is in the grip of a most desperate food crisis, with millions of people dying of starvation every year. This crisis is partly of production and partly of distribution, but people are dying of starvation. The most careful scrutiny of the facts of population increase cannot fail to convince all those who study them that if the birth rate cannot be reduced, the death rate in the world must rise sharply. Disease, war and famine, the three horsemen, are the only available means of population regulation if people in all nations refuse to bring births and deaths into harmony.

You could properly comment that Canada is so small that the irresponsible reproduction of her 20 million means almost nothing to the total number of people in the world, and you would be probably right. I would ask, however, that we examine our role, as world citizens who enjoy very special opportunities, and urge the necessity of directing our affairs so as best to discharge these opportunities and responsibilities.

We grow more food than we use in some of the richest lands in the world and thus can contribute to the world's food supply; we are innovators in agriculture, in technology and in social organization; and we have the ideals and the opportunity to demonstrate the harmony that can exist between a highly developed nation and the environment in which it lives. I must ask, therefore, will more Canadians add to the total world's food supply beyond the increase in our new mouths? Can a more populous Canada do a better job of encouraging the production, preservation and provision of more food in other lands? Can we, more populous, conduct ourselves so that we do not continue to destory the potential of our own land to provide for us? Will more people make it more or less likely that we will reduce the present input of harmful chemicals into the air, the soil, and the water that are the sources of our riches? With more people can we manage our activities toward the native plants and animals under our care so that we do not permanently impoverish the world as a consequence of our being?

I come to the inevitable conclusion that, despite the fact that we live in one of the least heavily populated parts of the world, on a person per acre basis, and enjoy a position among the wealthier nations, our role will not be improved by internal policies designed to produce a steady increase in numbers. Better by far to devote ourselves to exploring the mechanisms whereby we can, with our form of government, reduce or eliminate the proportion of our citizens whose share of the resources is so small that it scarcely meets the needs of survival. Better also to explore effective ways in which we can continue to fulful the aspirations of men without degrading the living environment. There is social, political, economic, and technological exploration to be done of benefit to all people. What more effective start than demonstrating here the patterns whereby the critical equation of numbers can be balanced and an economic and ecological conscience developed. So I will state my policies as I come to them.

Number one, stabilize our population. No other target of Canadian internal policy exceeds in importance that of our policy toward population growth. The nature of this policy and the effectiveness of its expression will influence almost everything else we plan for ourselves, as well as our ability to contribute to those less fortunate. But no matter what our attitudes toward increased numbers of Canadians, no action we can take today will make itself felt in time to avoid continued increase for many years ahead, with the problems that increase compounds, even though they will not be as serious for us as they are for the majority of the world.

Let me turn to the second question, which arises from the first. We all know that the land surface of Canada cannot be measured in acres per person. That is ridiculous. It is unique in many ways that can have powerful influence upon people and upon the way we must conduct

146

ourselves. One can see in our system little evidence that we accept the reality that only a very small part of Canada can be effectively used for food production. Yet this small part is our trust to the world's hungry as mankind desperately fights famine. We should use this to buy time for them while they put their house in order and bring their birth rate down. It seems logical to me that if food is, and will probably continue to be, the limiting factor on human numbers and human values, we should be making every effort to dedicate to food production every possible source.

In this context what have been the consequences of our attitudes up to now? Year after year I watch my City of Vancouver sprawling onto the richest delta lands of the Fraser River. I see the small towns of the Okanagan Valley spreading at the expense of rich orchard lands; I see the Niagara Peninsula disappearing under tons of concrete and asphalt. Everywhere we turn we see the consequence of an economic policy that does not recognize as the number one priority the production of crops on crop lands. The strategic location of towns and transportation would lead inevitably to some encroachment, but in places—and Vancouver is an example—there are thousands of acres of non-agricultural or marginal land suitable for homesites and industry. The only consideration now seems to be the easiest profit to the developer.

As a second important policy position then I would urge a review of our basis for priorities of land use, and the establishment of a more broadly applicable system of zoning for most appropriate use. The implications of such a policy would be far reaching and would introduce economic considerations demanding ingenuity and firm resolve. After all our economy is based upon continuous increase—that can't go on forever—let's decide now that land can be permanently allocated to agricultural or other low density use on the basis of maximum stability. Failure to take this step will see steady erosion of our food—producing potential.

It is already apparent that as food becomes scarce certain components become limiting before others. The pathetic plight of the protein deficient millions in the over-populated, undeveloped areas of the world needs no further elaboration here. We see these ghastly pictures of protein deficient children almost daily in the news magazines of the world. Not only is there a priority for food over other products of the land in the world of the immediate future, but the demand for animal protein exceeds all else, and this brings me to the plight of our rivers.

The Fraser River is probably the greatest fish carrying river in the world. In one magnificent harvest a very few years ago 22 million individual fish of one species out of the five was added to the world's food supply. These are fish that annually migrate from the vast reaches of the

147

Pacific Ocean, where they have grown fat and developed their protein on organisms that man cannot use for food. This resource can be contributing perpetually not only to the economy of Canada, but to the world's store of edible animal protein. Yet we have responsible engineers repeatedly seriously urging us that the river be dammed near its mouth for hydro-electric power. It is admitted that this would mean the extermination of most of the salmon stocks. Nevertheless we are shown that the optimum economic benefit is said to point to the conversion of the river for energy, not protein. On this occasion the salmon interests have so far prevailed, but not because of any firmly held national policy of priority, and the threat continues. And once a stock of these creatures is destroyed it is gone forever.

The time can clearly be foreseen when the feeding of potential human food to livestock will no longer be tolerable. The ninety percent loss of energy that transpires when you do this is too great. We could well adopt policies that would set out agricultural researchers to exploring means of raising our animal protein on the products of land not suitable for direct production of human food in other sources.

My policy number three then is priority of animal protein in suitable rivers and inshore seas. Would it not be reasonable to recommend the adoption of policies that firmly establish the primacy of protein in the highly productive areas of our rivers and inshore seas. Such a policy would point cleary to behaviour designed to maintain the ecological health of these waters.

There are several reasons for deciding to curb the increase in people here, and the global food shortage is only one of these. There can be few among you that are not daily made aware of the inadequacy or unwillingness of our present economy to provide enough resources for the education of the young. The demographic facts are that the age group in the most expensive stage of their lives (6 to 26) is the largest unit in our population. The producing age group is finding itself hard put to meet the costs of adequately preparing the young to undertake their parts in the continuing tasks and the completely novel roles that will emerge nationally and internationally. Every generation faces a new future, with uncharted courses to be pioneered. The only thing we can be certain of is the increasing rates of change in both internal and external systems, and opting out won't alter this one iota. Thus the task of the educator becomes increasingly demanding of new ideas, new attitudes, new forms. The chance of meeting these challenges would be greatly improved if some relief from burgeoning numbers could really permit us to devote our total innovative energies in this field to the task of quality, rather than to the continuous preoccupation with numbers, translated into acres of new facilities and dollars per square foot.

I and hundreds of my colleagues find it discouraging to spend untold hours converting each new undergraduate in Arts into 12 square feet of lecture rooms, and each potential scientist or faculty member into another cypher. These men and these women could turn their minds to the tasks they really enjoy, designing and participating in better, more ingenious, more sensitive, more humane education, were they just permitted to do so. So my policy number four: educators should be permitted to educate and should be provided the resources and encouragement to do it to the best of their ability.

I comment now with some trepidation on the sociological consequences of burgeoning numbers in the developed countries, as I pretend no expert knowledge in this area. However, as I read the message of today and of the recent past, I find no escape from the conclusion that more people, crowded into larger cities at greater densities and living more complicated lives, inevitably means a greater degree of interdependence between these city people, and this, in turn, means more regimentation of the individual, inevitably more ways in which the individual must abrogate his personal freedom of action in the best interests of the total society. The many corollaries to more people can only steepen the curve of this change. So if you regard the limitations of your freedom of action as contrary to your vision of the kind of life you would like to live, the conclusion is obvious.

So, as you may follow the irresponsible dictates of your primal sex urges, clothed only in the pretence that you are demonstrating your freedom to do as you please, the outcome may well be a noose drawn somewhat tighter around your other freedoms. I don't anticipate that the remark will cause you to pause long on the brink of ecstasy—but it should! I might issue the old adage, if you can't be good be careful.

Another population-based concern is the massive alteration that technological man imposes on the air, water, soil, and living creatures of this planet. I do not refer only to the rate at which we use the physical and biological resources, because all animals use the resources of their environment. It is part of the way of life. I refer rather to the multitudes of ways in which we either reduce the capability of the earth to produce for our use as it might, and to the intrusion of our effluents and our activities in ways that so alter the environment that many millions of people find their lives impoverished and their futures put in jeopardy. So my policy number five: the integrity of the environment must be maintained. Let me now return to the Fraser River and its salmon. We find a new danger threatening the integrity of our fresh water as a burgeoning human population continues to use them for sewage disposal. The

149

migratory fishes coming in from the ocean make their homing run to their parent stream following infinitesimal dilutions of critical chemicals. Now I pause in admiration at the capacity of any salmon entering the Fraser River to detect in this excretic broth that now flows between the river banks, the sources of their homing. There is no knowing when the critical level of pollution will be exceeded, but once it is that river will be as effectively closed to salmon as if it had a dam across it. And this is but a single example of the way we are treating our rivers all over the North American continent as open sewers.

However, this is only a very minor aspect of one of the most omnipresent and pervasive ways in which man is disrupting the environment and endangering his own health. One of the most dramatic differences between the poorly developed and the technological cultures is in the nature of their wastes. While the folk culture has wastes largely of a biological nature—the advanced cultures produce vast amounts of hard wastes and of poisonous materials.

Our action toward the disposal of fluid and gaseous wastes is based upon the principles of dilution. This is a delightfully simple and logical concept but it is very frequently false. It reads like this: if we have wastes to be removed, even if their concentrated form is harmful to living material, we can assume that if we merely dilute them to harmlessness we can dump them into our rivers or lakes or oceans. Our attitude toward the air is no different. There is increasing evidence, however, that the principle of dilution is often false where biologically active chemicals are concerned.

We have only two of these chemicals that we have really studied thoroughly. I refer to DDT and to radioactive by-products. In both of these instances it has been clearly shown that, rather than continuing dilution to inconsequence, biological concentration is what really occurs. The introduction of these materials into the life chemistry of the smallest categories of food organisms leads to gradual and progressive concentration up the food chain, until the summit creatures, in the case of DDT, perish or become sterile through the accumulation of the chemical.

In this way we are watching the steady disappearance of many of the fish-eating and flesh-eating creatures, irreplaceable biological treasures of our land. At the same time it has been shown that the caribou of our Arctic tundras are carrying very heavy loads of radioactive materials. So far we do not know that their lives have been shortened or the rate of harmful mutations increased—but then we have not really looked. It is pertinent to add that man is a summit creature in the food chain concept. It is possible to contemplate the increased human sterility with some equanimity, but it is not possible to regard increasing human ill-health in the same light. Increased mutation on the other hand would be tragic.

150

My policy six then is, fresh unpolluted water must be regarded as a prime commodity. Our rivers are not the cleansers of the nation. One can see ahead desperate political struggles on this continent for access to water, pure water for the use of people and their crops. I can leave to your imagination the alternatives open to us in Canada when this state has been reached as in an overcrowded continent.

However, there are more issues than these: as the products of our factories, farms, and bathrooms pour into the water bodies on which we must depend for our own use and for our food and recreation; as the air we breathe becomes steadily less suitable for this purpose; and as levels of soil contamination rise. The environment for many forms of plants and animals is altered in many ways, often so subtle as to be undetectable, until consequence is so far removed from cause that the relationship escapes us.

The details of our spreading pollution of the environment are added to almost daily and there is neither time nor need for me to go into them here. It is an unfortunate fact of life that in our society well-documented warnings are seldom heeded and only crisis situations lead to action. By this time, however, recovery is unlikely. This is certainly applicable to the steady destruction of the environment by our waste products. Recent nation-wide conferences on water quality have introduced this aspect of the problem to the public sector, and here and there across Canada some courageous politicians are seriously trying to reverse the trend. This is devoted almost entirely, however, to sewage and factory effluent and has not yet turned to the more serious problems involving biocide chemicals used in agriculture, horticulture, forestry, and highway maintenance.

The solutions to the many facets of the huge and rapidly increasing impact of environmental degradation by the waste products of our society must be sought vigorously, and as they emerge must be made part of our continuing national policy. No other aspect of our behaviour can have such widespread impact on the potential that Canada will maintain for both rich, varied, and satisfying lives for our people, along with the maintenance of the native organisms.

Finally, I must return to one of the most distinctive attributes of a developed country—the greatly diversified opportunities for recreation available to us. This is an entire subject in itself, and we have time but to salute it in passing. Almost certainly the greater part of man's leisure will find its expression in city-based things and activities. We have been made aware almost dramatically by recent writers in the "new culture" that there are now millions whose total interest rests with the urban environment. They have not the slightest interest, I am told—I can't imagine it—in wild land or the recreation that is to be found there. It is a fact, however, that the growth of outdoor types of recreation exceeds all others. Parks, wilderness, wild rivers, wildlife refuges, fishing areas, ski resorts, and a host of other forms of expression recognize this search by man for the diversified physical and spiritual refreshment that is to be found so abundantly in the wild state.

We have made a good start in the preservation and management of such areas in Canada. Much more needs to be done if we are to maintain quality in these opportunities in face of the degrading impact of numbers and the blight of our, I mean your, garbage. Those that seek wilderness solitude should find it, those that delight in unspoiled nature have a right to expect that it will still be there, near at hand as well as in the uninhabitable reaches of our land. And those that seek merely the revivifying and interesting contact with majestic scenery, without strenuous physical exertion, must continue to find it in suitable settings. Here lies another challenge to those that search for policies to guide our society in its constant, confused and often troubled search for national expression of a way of life distinctively ours.

So my policy number seven then: one of the greatest attributes of Canada is unspoiled landscapes for the recreational, cultural and scientific enrichment of our lives; our policy should be to guard these values from erosion by careless, ignorant, or avaricious people.

We have two roles, two distinct but interdependent responsibilities. One of these might be superficially designated as self-centred, because it is concerned primarily with how we react toward the environment of Canada. If we conduct ourselves with due concern for the long term well-being of the soil, waters, air, and wild creatures of Canada we will have provided the basis upon which a rich and healthy culture can be built, and at the same time, I am convinced, the social revolution that must precede and accompany such a complete change in our philosophy of man's relation to his surroundings will inevitably change us in other ways also.

A people that is totally oriented to conduct itself so as to preserve the integrity of the basic ingredients of its well-being will inevitably be more directly, practically, and sensitively concerned with the needs and responsibilities of all its peoples. This may sound utopian and probably is, but without dreams of better things there will be no advances. When we have moved in the directions I suggest we will not only have a better environment in which to live lives of broader and more edifying experience, but we will have learned how to solve some of our besetting social problems. What is even more important, we will have learned that investment in the continuation of these values of the environment are worthwile in every sense. Similarly, that investment of time, energy,

152

genuinely creative resourcefulness, and the necessary resources in the well-being of the total human society, can be just as truly a worthwhile investment. Every member of a society in which it is impossible to respond effectively to the genuine need of its less fortunate members is paying a price in terms of health, happiness, restricted opportunities for living, or in other more subtle ways.

As indicated earlier, we also have an external responsibility. It rests in developing our capacity to use our technological ability, our social ingenuity, our ecological and social conscience, and a portion of our wealth to help people of other nations to move along their own paths towards the goals that all men seek.

Aldous Huxley says: "Only when we get into our collective heads that the basic problem confronting twentieth century man is an ecological one will our policies improve. Do we propose to live on the planet in symbiotic harmony with our environment? Or, preferring to be wantonly stupid, shall we choose to live like murderous and suicidal parasites that kill their host and so destory themselves."

What I hear on our campuses today are the cries of a new conscience—a rapidly swelling tide of people of all ages are getting new visions of what can be and what they feel should not be in this part of the world and elsewhere. Our challenge in framing Canadian internal policy is to identify these new and more acceptable goals, to discover new routes and new mechanisms for reaching them. The task is complex and of great urgency—but the call that is rising is for leadership, for the opportunity to participate in actions that will hold more visible promise, in which one major component is what Aldo Leopold calls an ecological conscience, another is a demonstrated concern for those in distress.

"CANADA'S ROLE IN THE WORLD POPULATION CRISIS"
Hugh L. Keenleyside

Hugh Llewellyn Keenleyside was born in Toronto in 1898, married in 1924, and is the father of four children. He studied at the University of British Columbia, and then at Clark University where he was awarded the Ph.D. in history. After teaching in American universities for a number of years he joined the faculty of his alma mater.

Dr. Keenleyside entered diplomatic and government service in 1928. Some of his positions were as follows. He was First Secretary in the Canadian Mission to Japan from 1929 to 1936. Later he became Assistant Under-Secretary of State for External Affairs in Ottawa. From 1944 to 1947 he served as Ambassador to Mexico. He was appointed Deputy Minister of the Canadian Department of Mines and Resources. He joined the United Nations first as Chief of the UN Technical Assistance Mission to Bolivia and then continued as Director-General of the United Nations Technical Assistance Administration. In 1959 he returned to Canada and was chairman of the British Columbia Hydro and Power Authority until June, 1969.

At various times Dr. Keenleyside has served on national and international government councils and commissions on defence, economics, Arctic research, atomic energy, etc. In addition he has served in civic organizations such as the Canadian Welfare Council and the YMCA, on boards of directors of Canadian businesses, and as a member of the Board of Directors of Resources for the Future.

Throughout his busy life Dr. Keenleyside has maintained academic connections and has published articles and books, the title of one of the latter being "International Aid". He has received a number of honorary doctoral degrees.

As I have been flatteringly described on the programme as an "economist", I think that I should make at least a brief reference to the interesting contribution to our discussions made earlier by Colin Clark. I have known Dr. Clark and have been well acquainted with his views on the population problem for more than 20 years. If I say that while I greatly admire many of Dr. Clark's activities, my comments will be firmly based on the assumption that he is wrong, I hope that he will not charge me, as

155

he did certain others, with the "sin of pride."

I should like to take time to endorse and underline many of the things said by my distinguished colleague from British Columbia, Dr. Cowan. But I am afraid that I should only dull the effect of his persuasive eloquence. Let me say, however, that in spite of my direct interest in hydro-electric power, I am not one of those who wishes to dam the Fraser River!

My subject is Canada's role in the World Population Crisis. Actually, I don't need 25 minutes for this task. The topic can be summarized in 25 seconds. Until a short time ago Canada had no policy except a sort of dumb but obstinate resistance to doing anything, or even of encouraging others to do what was and is obviously necessary. Recently, influenced by public opinion at home and a changing atmosphere abroad, our delegates to meetings of international agencies have been allowed to speak, in low and carefully restrained whispers, in favour of programmes designed to assist requesting governments to deal with their spawning populations. But we have given no leadership; taken no initiatives.

Perhaps, even after the discussions during this Teach-In, it may be asked why should we in Canada be alarmed about the population problem? We have plenty of room. Other countries can take care of their food needs by using new agricultural methods: the new seeds, the new fertilizers, the new techniques that are now available. Humanity has faced crises before, and has survived. Why all the excitement? Relax and everything will be all right, Jack.

The answer is short and simple; everything will *not* be all right.

There has been a general disposition in this conference to avoid undue detail in what has been referred to as "the numbers game." But the essential facts are, first, that whereas it took millions of years from the beginning of the human species to about the middle of the nineteenth century for mankind to reach a total of one billion persons, since then, in a little over 100 years, that number has multiplied three and one-half times.

Second, not only has the world population increased in this phenomenal way but the *rate of increase* is still rising. Every time the United Nations provides an estimate the percentage is higher.

And, third, the rapid growth of population is making it impossible to achieve the kind of economic and social progress in the underdeveloped areas of the world that is imperatively necessary if we are to alleviate the grim misery that afflicts over half of all the people on earth.

In spite of the efforts that have been made in the years since the end of the Second World War there has, in fact, been very little progress in most of these countries. In some ways the situation has grown worse. For example, we tend to take it for granted that, because of the work being done in the provision of schools by national governments, and the contributions made by UNESCO, and some of the great Foundations, the handicap of illiteracy will soon be removed. But the fact is that every year there is *an increase of over 30 million illiterates*. And since 1945 the total number of human beings living in the degradation of poverty and ignorance has grown by over one billion.

The· production of food is not keeping ahead of increasing populations. Last year, in 1967, the per capita food production in Latin America, Africa, and the Far East was less than it was before the Second World War. No conceivable increase in production will solve the problems of proliferating humanity as long as unrestricted births continue to add to the sum of human needs, and to impede all efforts to meet them.

It is against this background that I suggest we should look at the Canadian record.

The World Health Organization which was established at the end of the Second World War was thrown into a furious turmoil at one of its first sessions by a proposal that it should help requesting governments to introduce plans to limit their population growth. (Incidentally, the Director General of WHO, who tried to get action on this proposal, was the Canadian Dr. Brock Chisholm, certainly one of the most remarkable men of his generation.) But what did Canada do about this eminently sensible proposal? *The Canadian delegates threatened to withdraw unless the matter was dropped! It was dropped.*

When the subject came up again in debates in the World Health Organization, and in UNICEF, and in the United Nations itself, the Canadian representatives were usually silent, or engaged in double talk. If votes were taken we usually took a negative line, or abstained. This was one of the reasons that Canada became known in United Nations circles as "the great abstainer." (The title had no relation to the social habits of our delegates.) In recent years the Canadian position has been somewhat modified and, according to an official interpretation, "Canada has supported measures designed to give the United Nations the authority to respond to requests for advice and assistance for developing countries on population questions." This is true but it is also true that the Canadian support has been in such pianissimo terms as to be barely audible. And the support has been almost exclusively verbal. For example: in December 1966 *twelve heads of states* presented to the Secretary General of the United Nations a declaratiqn urging that immediate and effective action be taken to deal with the population problem.

The Prime Minister of Canada was not one of the twelve.

Then the original signers asked other world leaders to join them in their anxiety that something should be done. By December 1967 *thirty* heads of states had signed. Among them were the Prime Ministers or Presidents of Australia, New Zealand, India, Japan, the Netherlands, Norway, Pakistan, Sweden, Denmark, Great Britain, and the United States.

But not the Prime Minister of Canada.

Or again in July 1967 U Thant established a *Trust Fund for Population Activities* and invited Governments, organizations, and individuals to contribute. In this way the Secretary General hoped to obtain a little more freedom of action to promote progress in this field. Within a year 11 governments had responded favourably, and just under a million dollars had been provided.

But nothing came from Canada.

If Canada has acted in a generally negative way when population matters were discussed in the international agencies, our record in our bilateral programmes of international aid has been even worse. This, of course, is not surprising. Canadian law still makes the provision of birth control information and facilities a criminal offence, and we can hardly provide direct aid abroad when we prohibit it at home. In view of recent developments this situation may soon change. To quote again from the official interpretation referred to above: "The Government has indicated *its intention to re-examine* those provisions of the Criminal Code relating to contraception and *if the proposed amendments to the Criminal Code are approved* Ministers *would be in a position to consider the advisability* of introducing family planning programmes into Canada's bilateral programmes."

I am sure that you will recognize the tremendous sense of urgency and of dynamic determination that characterizes these official statements!!

Of course, we know that many of the Canadian participants in international aid programmes recognize the imperative need of action on population and would be glad to act if permitted to do so.

The most hopeful development in Canadian policy occurred less than a month ago. Robert S. McNamara, in his first major address as head of the World Bank, said that in future aid to underdeveloped countries should be made dependent, in part at least, on the willingness of those countries themselves to do something effective about limiting their population growth. To the general astonishment of most observers the Canadian representative at the Bank meeting, the Honourable Edgar Benson, in a major speech specifically endorsed the McNamara proposal. When queried about this announcement Ottawa officials said, to quote the Canadian Press, "Benson was not announcing any new specific Canadian policy in linking birth control programs to development aid. They said it has been acknowledged for years that a high birth rate is one of the factors holding back economic progress in underdeveloped countries." *This is a pretty example of the official capacity to say something that is technically true but really conveys a false impression.* If it has been acknowledged for years why has Canada not said so before—and why have we done nothing about it? However, we should be grateful that our Government is now hinting that it is going to do something sensible even if it refuses to admit the obvious fact that it is, for Canada, something new.

In an earlier session of the Teach-In a questioner asked Professor Stycos (who incidentally made what I considered a most admirable address) what, as individual Canadians, we could do about the situation we all face. Professor Stycos, being an American, was really too polite in his reply. Let me make some suggestions: Let us assume that the Canadian Government, by its promise of action on the Criminal Code, and by Mr. Benson's statement on international aid, is giving us signals that it is prepared at last to act intelligently on the population issue. There are certain specific things that we can ask them to do and support them in doing.

First, we should insist that Parliament must wipe out the imbecile prohibition that has stained our Criminal Code. It is violated a million times a day—it is evil in itself, and it inhibits our plans to assist both ourselves and others.

Second, so far as we usefully can, we should assist those who are trying to change ecclesiastical attitudes, attitudes which have resulted in an appalling record of personal tragedy, have caused incalculable human suffering, and have been one of the major obstacles to social and economic progress throughout the world. (In this connection it might be noted that the recent Papal Encyclical on birth control was addressed to "men of good will." Perhaps we should interpret this to mean that women can do as they like!)

Third, we should radically increase our aid to the underdeveloped countries. By our Government's own and repeated confession, less than one-half of one percent of our G.N.P. is not our fair share. Our contributions lag well behind those of a number of other countries, including some that are much less affluent than ourselves. But I agree that in increasing our aid we should, at the same time, insist that recipient governments face their own responsibilities including the responsibility of encouraging their people in family planning. We should join the McNamara band.

As long as conditions of general ignorance, poverty and the manifold forms of injustice, degradation, and hopelessness continue to oppress over half the people of the world, so long as sexual indulgence is the only luxury available to vast numbers of human beings, so long will populations increase and human misery, with all its potential of local strife and international conflict, remain to endanger ourselves and our world.

Fourth, we should urge WHO, UNICEF and the United Nations itself, to increase enormously their concern with this aspect of their duties. That those who guide their programmes are willing and indeed anxious to take such action is no secret. But they cannot act except as their governing bodies decree. We should ensure that, so far as Canada is concerned, the required support is not lacking.

Finally, why should Canada not devote a significant amount of money to research in the field of population control? We have a large—though not large enough—and highly competent national research establishment. Nothing that our scientists are doing can compare in potential for human happiness with the solution of the problem of birth control. We shall never remove the dangers of excess population until we find something better than present techniques and use every available device to change present attitudes. Neither the rhythm method, the pill, sterilization, abortion, nor the various mechanical and chemical procedures so far developed, will ever be used except by a small proportion of those who must be *converted to desire*, and *assisted to effect*, a rational control over the number of their progeny. Present methods are too uncertain, are too expensive, are too complicated, or require too great a sophistication on the part of the users to be generally effective. And here I have a specific proposal to offer.

Would it not make sense, in fact, would it not be a step towards national sanity to close down the Suffolk experimental station where we are developing new horrors for chemical and bacteriological warfare, and devote the money thus saved to a search for methods of population control which would add dignity, hope and decency to human life? Or let's forego a couple of bombers and divert the millions now being senselessly squandered, to this good cause. In what other way could Canada do as much for human happiness and peace as by discovering an effective means of solving this problem? Even if we failed, the fact that we had tried would add a new distinction to the title of Canadian.

As a sidelight to this connection and as an illustration of the way in which the world is prostituting the talents of its scientists let us remember that today in the United States and Canada over one hundred universities—universities!—are engaged in research on nuclear, biological and bacteriological warfare. This example of human perversion is further illustrated by the recent incident in Washington where a woman scientist was awarded the Army Medal for Distinguished Service for developing a fungus that would destroy the rice plant.

160

What will happen if Canada and the other nations do not take the kind of sensible action that is imperative to solve the population problem? Well, it is possible of course that some natural law, which has not yet been discovered, will bring into operation an automatic check on the rate of population growth. There is no evidence to support the belief that there is any such law, but like Mr. Micawber we can always hope that something will turn up.

It is possible that some great national catastrophe or a long series of major calamities (famines, floods, epidemics, and so on) may drastically reduce the human population. But it hardly seems sensible to rely on, and even less to look forward hopefully to, such a solution.

As Professor Cole suggested, perhaps the increasing use of nuclear energy and of radioactive substances generally may grow to such dimensions that it will effectively interfere with the reproductive capacity of human beings. It is not so many years ago that the then head of our Chalk River plant said that if he was a young man hoping to raise a family he would not live near Chalk River.

But, failing such accidental and unforeseeable natural solutions, more direct and specific methods will have to be adopted in the years ahead if we refuse to use our intelligence and knowledge and initiative to control population growth.

After the first session of this Teach-In, as I was walking back to my hotel along Bloor Street, I heard a young lady just behind me announcing to her companions in a loud and shrill voice that population growth could never be stopped because sexual intercourse (that was not the term she used) "is too much fun." Now in her own vulgar and illiterate little way this young woman was stating a fact of great sociological and demographic importance. Preaching restraint just won't work.

It is true that a few days ago Dr. Chandrasehkar was quoted by the Canadian Press as proposing that all married couples in India should refrain from sexual intercourse for one year. This, he said, would do enormous good to the individuals and to the country. As a propaganda ploy to draw attention to the importance of the population problem this was excellent. But realistically not even the people of India could be expected to display that measure of self-restraint. And, if by some miracle they did, it would probably just mean that every couple in the country would have a baby the following year!

As indicated earlier, the threatening tragedy is not far ahead. If present trends continue, children of young people in this audience will be faced with the necessity of enforcing birth control through the compulsory sterilization of a vast number of their fellow human beings. Or, perhaps, if Canadians are no longer members of the world's ruling elite, the sterilization will be enforced against them!

Alternatively of course your children or grandchildren may decide to let the babies be born and get rid of them afterwards. Perhaps by early in the twenty-first century it may be possible to transport them to some other planet. Or the babies, particularly girl babies, could be exposed as the Spartans once did. Or members of less-favoured racial or national or religious groups could be subjected to some process such as Hitler's "final solution" for the Jews. (There might, of course, be some difference of opinion as to who should be selected for such a process of elimination!)

Even after the brutalizing effects of 40 or 50 more years of population growth it would probably still be impracticable to adopt Dean Swift's "modest proposal" that babies, particularly babies of poor people, should be fattened and eaten!

All of this sounds horrible—but the prospect is horrible unless we act both sensibly and soon.

In this generation we face the two greatest dangers in human history—nuclear weapons which could wipe out all humanity, and population growth which, unchecked, will make life unbearable. *The bomb and the womb must both be controlled.* Both *can* be controlled but only if we decide to use the intelligence, the wisdom and the initiative which we possess but so seldom effectively employ.

Of course it may be that humanity is merely a type of bacteria that infects this tiny planet in a distant corner of the great universe we apprehend but do not understand. Perhaps like other bacterial infections we may be destined to run our little course and swiftly disappear. But this may not be our *nature*, our *function* or our *fate*. At least we should not contribute by design, omission or default to such a drab and squalid conclusion to the story of our race. But our eventual epitaph will record a different fortune only if we now act to dispel the looming threat that we see, but have as yet done so little to avert. *It is time now for action.*

PLANNED PARENTHOOD:
BACKGROUND AND DEVELOPMENT IN SWEDEN

Thorsten Sjövall

Thorsten Sjövall (pronounced Shev-vahl) was born in Hälsingborg, Sweden in 1913. He studied medicine at Uppsala, with internships in psychiatry and internal medicine. He spent two years, 1949 to 1951, in Boston, Massachusetts working in psychiatry and psychoanalysis. From 1952 he has practiced as a psychiatrist at Stockholm's Mental Health Clinic and now is head of psychiatric services there.

Dr. Sjövall has participated in a number of professional, civic and international organizations. He is or has been president of the Swedish Association of Sex Education, the Swedish Psychoanalytic Society, the Swedish Society for Group Psychotherapy. He holds executive positions on various committees of the International Planned Parenthood Federation.

Dr. Sjövall has published many papers on psychiatry, psychosomatic medicine, psychosexology and parenthood planning.

One important background for Swedish population policy is the fact that the first census was taken as far back as 1749 and that Sweden since has achieved the réputation of having one of the most accurate records of vital statistics in the world. Thus population development has been more closely followed through a more extended period of time in Sweden than in most other countries. Yet this did not result in anything like a determined population policy until the 1930s.

During the first 30 years of this century about half a million people out of a mean population of about 5.5 million emigrated from Sweden. During the next 30-year period the net number of people who emigrated was less than 300,000. At the beginning of the 1930s the immigration was greater than the emigration and the number of immigrants has shown a definite tendency to increase ever since.

In the meantime birthrates kept falling rather steadily to reach a figure somewhat over 14 per 1000 in the early 1930s. In 1935 the well known couple Alva and Gunnar Myrdal published their book *Population Crisis*. The alarming message of this book was that an extermination of the Swedish population was predictable if steps were not taken to counteract prevailing trends in population development. It inaugurated the first period of active population policy in terms of an extensive social reform work aiming at family support and an increase of birth rates.

However, during the last three decades the picture of falling birth rates and increasing immigration has essentially remained. Social reforms and an increasing standard of living have not turned the downward trend of birth rates. A slight increase in the earlier half of the 1960s was due mainly to the "baby boom" age groups of the war, and the years after, having reached fertile age. When in 1960 the birth rate struck a bottom record of 13.7 some concern for the development was again uttered. Since then, however, mass media have paid increasing attention to the world population situation and its implications, perhaps contributing to the fact that very little has been said in the present public debate to the effect that any particular efforts for speeding up population growth would be warranted. It seems justified to state that under the influence of increasing knowledge and responsible recognition of international population problems, a growing opinion, at least in the younger generation and among intellectuals, holds that eventual under-population problems whould be solved by immigration rather than by stepping up national birth rates.

Thus, the general opinion on population problems has gradually shifted from a concern for national under-population problems to a growing interest and engagement in the international over-population situation. Therefore it seems appropriate for me, also from a historical point of view, to start with a description of the internal situation, pertaining to population policy in Sweden and then try to show how this has developed into the present activities on the international scene.

The Internal Situation
I.   The voluntary planned parenthood movement.
It is only fair to begin with the Swedish voluntary planned parenthood movement, because in many respects it has been leading the way in creating the kind of climate which may be designated as characteristically Swedish in the development of activities within this whole area. To understand this development, it is essential to know that it has proceeded, as it were, from below and upwards through the different strata of society, and not the other way around as it must in most developing countries today.

Although it has obvious relations to population policy, particularly in modern propaganda, it is noteworthy that the planned parenthood movement, in Sweden as in other countries pioneering in this field, did not start on a population policy basis but entirely for social welfare reasons. The population aspects of the matter are a rather recent addition and have, as far as Sweden itself is concerned, never been of any importance, the national population situation being as described above. The social welfare origin of the Swedish voluntary parenthood movement is reflected in the name it was given when founded in 1933, the Swedish Association for Sex Education (RFSU). Now, 35 years later, when the importance of public motivation and sex education for a reasonable success in international parenthood planning work is generally recognized, we are happy to have had this name for our national organization from the start. It emphasizes a rather broad approach to the subject based on general sexological knowledge.

The original formulation of aims of the RFSU comprised such proposals as the introduction of sex education in all schools including universities, the legalization of instrumental contraception, which was more or less forbidden at the time, a broadening of the requisites for obtaining legal abortion and sterilzation, other law revisions and social reforms motivated by the findings of modern scientific sexology, and the establishment of centres for providing public advice and guidance in sexual matters. In the early years the main method of promoting these aims was thousands of public lectures given all over the country by the vivacious founder of the movement, Mrs. Elise Ottesen-Jensen. This illustrates the aforementioned type of work from below and upwards, which was strengthened by a close cooperation with the growing labour movement as well as various voluntary organizations for adult education. Later were added seminars and courses for certain target groups of the population such as doctors, teachers, youth leaders and, furthermore, publications such as pamphlets, books, and a periodical which first appeared under the name *The Sexual Issue* and later as the *Popular Journal on Psychology and Sexual Knowledge*.

These activities were met by reactions along the whole range from enthusiasm through scepticism to indignation. Battles were fought which had the good result of stimulating debate and making the movement known all over the country, eventually to make it even generally respected. The way was then open for the RFSU to act as a pressure group by submitting proposals directly to appropriate authorities.

During the first 25 years of its existence the RFSU had the satisfaction of seeing many of the aims put forward in its original programme being realized. Appropriate sex education was made compulsory by law for all age levels at public schools. Legal restrictions on advertising and selling contraceptives were repealed. Planned parenthood as a human right was accepted in principle by state authorities. So was the responsibility of these authorities to provide appropriate public services for contraceptive advice. The abortion law was reformed by several steps

165

towards increased liberalization, and the services for implementation of the law were taken over by the communities. After this the RFSU dropped the service for legal abortion applicants, which was the first of its kind in the country, from its clinical activities.

The original idea was for the RFSU to provide a nation-wide network of clinics for sexual and contraceptive advice through its local branch organizations. Since this responsibility has been recognized, at least in principle, by the official public health services, the RFSU retains only a couple of model clinics as a source of basic knowledge and experience for what is now felt as the main task of the organization, namely to provide expert information and proposals within the field of sexology and its social implications.

Mrs. Jensen was one of the founders and the RFSU one of the founder organizations of the International Planned Parenthood Federation (IPPF). Since then, mainly through the personal initiatives of Mrs. Jensen, the RFSU and later the Swedish nation have played a leading role in international planned parenthood work. When in 1960 the Canadian George Cadbury was elected Special Representative of the President of the IPPF for field work activities—the President at the time was Mrs. Jensen—he urged the national organizations of the IPPF to intensified efforts at stimulating their governments to increased investments in local and international planned parenthood activities. Mrs. Jensen immediately followed this suggestion and contributed considerably to get those activities started that today have given the Swedish government a leading position as a supporter of international planned parenthood work.

II.   General government policy and social reforms during the last 30 years.
Two seemingly contradictory lines of thought underlie the internal policy followed by the Swedish government during the last three decades. One is an increasing public awareness of the welfare and psycho-social aspects of sex, stimulated by the activities of the RFSU and aiming mainly at voluntary birth control and child-spacing. The other is a general concern for under-population, pronounced in the 1930s but then apparently rapidly disappearing. However, on the wave of this under-population concern a State Population Commission was appointed in 1935. During the following three years the commission released 17 printed publications as a result of which the Parliament decided on state loans for young couples' settling expenses, the establishment of maternal and child health centres, free obstetrical care, maternity allowances and increased tax deductions for families with children.

In 1941 a new State Population Committee was appointed which by

1947 had submitted another 19 printed publications. In 1942 and 1943 the Parliament made provisions for certain home services and decided on state allowances for day nurseries. In 1946 free meals and free educational material at schools were introduced, and also facilities for rest and recreation for mothers and children. In the following year the tax deduction for families with children was exchanged for cash allowances for each child.

In the 1950's the reform work was devoted mainly to the social insurance system. The general health insurance was improved, national basic pensions and supplementary pensions as well as cash allowances for students were introduced, and the cash allowances for children increased.

In the 1960s attention has been paid mainly to sex education, contraception, and abortion, and I shall return to these items separately in a moment.

While poverty comparable to that existing in the developing countries today was a stark reality in Sweden some 50 years ago and still constituted the main motivation for starting the voluntary planned parenthood movement in the early 1930s, the aim of modern family policy is rather the social adaptation and the psychic well-being of the individual in terms of providing optimal conditions for human intimacy and good family relationships within the entire population.

Under the conditions prevailing in Sweden today, birth control and family planning are neither matters of population control nor of material public welfare. They are, however, very definitely matters of social responsibility in terms of a widespread opinion that society should provide sufficient individual knowledge and preventive medical services to ensure that unwanted pregnancies are reduced to a minimum. The means envisaged for reaching this goal are mainly sex enlightenment, integrated at all levels of the public educational system, and contraceptive advice provided within the country-wide network of maternal and child health centres.

There is no significant opposition to this general policy. The state and community authorities recognize in principle their responsibilities as here outlined. Birth control and parenthood planning are regarded as important parts of preventive medicine by all political parties, but practical implementation of this policy is still lagging behind in that contraceptive services are not at all easily available in many rural districts. The RFSU keeps acting as a pressure group for increased official activities in this and other areas.

Differences of opinion in this field are quite conspicuous in every-day Swedish life as reflected in mass-media debates between radical groups on the one hand and defenders of religious or right-wing political views on the other. These controversies however, mainly deal with what, from an international point of view, must be considered as details such as what kind of sex information children should have at what age, the individual freedom of choice in abortion situations, etc.

III. Swedish abortion policy.

As is well known, the world today is divided in two parts with regard to abortion policy, one of which allows so-called free abortion, i.e., in principle at the discretion of the woman concerned, and another one which prescribes more or less severe restrictions for legal interruption of pregnancy. Sweden, being close to the demarcation line between those two blocks, has settled for a compromise legislation, but definitely sticks to the principle that contraception is preferable to abortion as a remedy against unwanted pregnancies.

Under the present law abortion is granted:

a) If childbirth would entail serious danger to life or health of a woman suffering from illness, a physical defect, or weakness as indicated by medical and medico-social authorities.

b) If there is reason to assume that childbirth and child care would seriously damage a woman's physical or psychic strength in view of her living conditions and other special circumstances.

c) If a woman has become pregnant as a result of rape, other criminal coercion, or incestuous sexual intercourse, or if she is mentally retarded, legally insane, or under fifteen years of age at the time of impregnation.

d) If there is reason to suspect that either parent of the expected child might transmit to the offspring hereditary insanity, imbecility, serious disease, or a serious physical handicap.

e) If there is reason to assume that the expected child will suffer from serious disease or deformity resulting from injury during fetal life.

As can be seen from this formulation of the law, particularly item b), it allows for considerable flexibility of interpretation. This has been the subject of an extensive public debate in the mass media, and this again has been reflected by large variations of the yearly number of applicants as well as in the percentage of applications granted by the National Board of Health and Welfare. Thus the number of applicants in 1960 was around 4,000, of which a little more than 60 percent were granted, whereas the corresponding figures for 1967 were over 10,000, of which more than 90 percent were granted. There seems to be no doubt that the fluctuation in the implementation of one and the same law is due to the expression of a public opinion supporting a more liberal interpretation of the law. This again has caused a demand for a new formulation of the law, securing a better uniformity of implementation, with due consideration to a prevailing public opinion demanding a greater decisive influence on the part of the women concerned. In 1965 a State Committee was appointed for this purpose, and a proposal is expected to be submitted to the Ministry of Justice in March, 1969.

In he meantime the RFSU, considering the fact that almost all applications at present are granted, has expressed the opinion that free abortion should be granted all applicants before the twelfth week of pregnancy.

It should be strongly emphasized that the Swedish abortion law is, in principle, considered applicable only to residents in Sweden. Only an insignificant number of all those women in distress coming to Sweden from all parts of the world in the hope of having a legal interruption can be helped the way they have anticipated.

IV.   Swedish contraceptive policy.

The legal ban on advertising and purchasing contraceptives was repealed in 1938. Since then there has been an extensive propaganda for contraception, particularly on the part of the RFSU, in accordance with the principle that this is the method of choice for avoiding unwanted pregnancies. The main methods recommended and used were diaphragms and condoms until, in the mid-60s, orals and IUDs were legally accepted as contraceptives. The orals have proved to be extremely attractive to the Swedish population, every fifth woman of fertile age being estimated to be on them at present. The IUDs have been much less popular and are used by an estimated number of some 20,000 women today. The condom has retained its position as a widely preferred contraceptive, whereas the number of diaphragm users dropped considerably after the appearance of the orals. Orals are provided by medical prescription only, and instructions for medical supervision of users are issued by the National Board of Health and Welfare.

In principle, contraceptive advice should be provided by the nation-wide network of maternal and child health centres. This has not worked out too well in practice. On the request of the RFSU, the National Board of Health and Welfare has recently appointed a committee with the instruction of submitting to the Board a plan for the improvement of this service on a nation-wide scale.

One measure of the efficiency of planned parenthood services in any one country is the total number of abortions in that country, provided that legal abortion, as is the case in Sweden, is not accepted as a recommendable method of birth control. Obviously there is then an inverse relationship between such efficiency and the number of abortions.

169

By this token the situation in Sweden is a rather favourable one, perhaps one of the best in the world, because on top of the 10,000 legal abortions in 1967 comes an estimated number of not more than 6000 illegal abortions, making a total number of abortions, giving a generous margin, of not more than 20,000. This figure should be seen against the number of live births in 1967, being 121,000. Compared to the estimated situation in most other countries, this is no doubt a favourable relationship. The reason for this, we hope and believe, is the general climate with regard to sexual matters in our country and the positive attitude towards public sex education.

V.   Sex education in Sweden.

No single factor has to such an extent contributed to Sweden's reputation of being a progressive country in sexual matters as has the fact that she is the first and so far the only country to have sex education at public schools as a legal requirement. This has been so since 1956. Again, however, implementation in practice has not amounted to the expectations reformers and law-makers or to those of an ever more sophisticated public. Teachers have been found to be badly prepared for this task. The guidance handbook for teachers on the subject, published by the National Board of Education in 1957, has been increasingly criticized for being old fashioned and moralizing.

These and other circumstances, among them demarches by the RFSU and other organizations to the Ministry of Education led, in 1964, to the appointment of a State Committee for a survey of the whole field of public sex education at school as well as the adult level. This committee is still at work.

External Policy

I.   General principles

I have not much space for Swedish external policy. I have felt it essential to present the internal situation in some detail, because it seems to me so important for understanding the Swedish role on the international scene. Sweden is a small country with no colonial past and well-known for her ambitions of taking a strictly neutral view on international affairs. She is also well-known for having achieved a peaceful and in many respects successful internal development that has given her a reputation of being the welfare state par excellence. These circumstances have no doubt contributed to the impression that the Swedish approach to these matters is comparatively soundly founded on ideological and humanitarian considerations. For instance, it is rightly assumed that Sweden would hesitate to advocate policies or methods for any other country that she would not be prepared to adopt at home.

Swedish foreign aid started by a comparatively small financial contribution to the United Nations Development Programme in 1950. A couple of years later the first bilateral project, a government-to-government agreement at the request of a particular developing country, was signed. Under the influence a growing international awareness of the urgency of the whole problem, particularly in view of the world population menace, expansion and organization of Swedish contributions to international development started to take shape in the early 60s.

In 1962 a government proposition, usually referred to as the international development bible, was accepted by the Parliament. In this document certain principles of policy, still essentially adhered to, were laid down. The one percent rule was adopted; i.e., development contributions should aim towards a total sum corresponding to one percent of the GNP. The multilateral type of aid was given a certain preference, and as far as bilateral aid is concerned, this should be provided at the request of the government in question only. Any project embarked upon should, preferably, have a maximal development effect; i.e., it should lead to an increased material welfare, better health, or expanded and more differentiated possibilities for education in the receiving country. Great importance was assigned to ethical principles of motivation such as promoting world peace, bridging the gap between rich and poor nations, furthering democratic ideas, and stimulating mutual collaboration rather than providing unilateral aid.

In that same year, 1962, a state department for organizing and channelling international development aid was created and this was, in 1965, expanded and reorganized into the present Swedish International Development Authority, SIDA. Financial appropriations amounted in the fiscal year 1967-8 to 80 million U.S. dollars, in the present year to 100 million U.S. dollars, and the request for the year 1968-69 is somewhat more than 125 million U.S. dollars. A continued yearly progression by this order would mean that the magic one percent mark would be reached by the mid 70s. The distribution of the total budget on multilateral and bilateral allocations is about half and half. This is a characteristic feature of Swedish policy, most other countries giving a much larger preference to bilateral investments. Sweden ranks, for instance, second only to the U.S. as a contributor to the UN Development Programme.

II.   International planned parenthood policy.

In a recent SIDA publication on the role of family planning in Sweden's development assistance programme, it is stated that there is a "strong

171

positive correlation between Sweden's assistance philosophy and the ideology underlying our domestic welfare policy." Swedish delegates at the UN General Assembly as well as at the UN Special Agencies have on several occasions during this decade appeared as spokesmen for the urgency of planned parenthood as an integrated part of any development programme. Both abroad and at home Sweden has thus been connected with a policy giving the highest priority to planned parenthood assistance.

This picture is not quite justified by the part of the total assistance budget actually allocated to planned parenthood projects. During the fiscal year 1962-63 this sum amounted only to 250,000 U.S. dollars. In 1967-68 it was four million U.S. dollars and in the present year it is nine million U.S. dollars, amounting to some 12 percent of the total assistance budget. However, the prospects are for this trend to continue, and the present policy of concentrating Swedish bilateral assistance to a few selected countries does not apply to planned parenthood activities.

Up to 1965 the Swedish government was the only one to operate official assistance programmes in the field of family planning. At present this is the case in Ceylon, Malaysia, Mauritius, Morocco, Pakistan, South Korea, Tunisia and Turkey. During 1968 it is expected that this list will be expanded to include India and a number of other countries in Asia as well as in Africa and Latin America.

When in 1962 the RFSU negotiated with government representatives about a financial contribution to the IPPF towards a family planning training institute in Singapore this was refused on the principle that the government would not support a voluntary organization. This policy has been changed, and in 1966 and 1967 the IPPF had a yearly allocation from the SIDA of 368,000 U.S. dollars. In 1968 this has been increased to about 500,000 U.S. dollars. Some two-thirds of this amount are without strings towards the IPPF general budget.

III.   Concluding remarks.

In conclusion I would like to emphasize that an outline of policies such as I have been trying to present here inevitably gives a rosier picture of the situation than is warranted by hard realities. Our internal reform programme towards a better solution of socio-sexological problems does not mean that old problems are entirely discarded or that new and serious problems are non-existent. This is indicated by the main title of this section of the Teach-In proceedings, "A Dilemma for Affluents." Likewise our development assistance programme is to an increasing extent being scrutinized by a wakening public opinion. It is criticized for being too slow, too parsimonious and too rigidly bureaucratic. A recently formed group of students for the study of international development problems has been quite active in this respect and demonstrated peacefully for a whole week against the last governmental proposition on the subject presented to the Parliament last spring.

As far as planned parenthood is concerned, I would like to quote a representative statement from the SIDA made in April 1967. It says: "The starvation in the developing countries is increasing because of the increase in population." This is the kind of statement with which informed and progressive people in Sweden today would not agree, because they feel that the whole problem is a lot more complicated than that. Another representative statement from the SIDA made in January 1968 runs as follows: "Our interest in promoting birth control is not accompanied by any comforting illusions about the problems involved in trying to stem the tide of population growth among illiterate, impoverished people. But it is felt that it would be rather unrealistic and indeed illogical to attempt to promote economic development without an accompanying effort to reduce births." This, I think, is a better expression of an informed opinion taking shape in Sweden today.

If I may end up by expressing a personal opinion it would be this. The importance of family planning, or as I prefer to call it, planned parenthood, has been grossly and propagandistically exaggerated as an outstanding remedy against the so-called population explosion. It has been underestimated if not neglected as something that by various methods might be presented to individuals as a means of ameliorating the kinds of human misery of which these individuals have a painful and direct experience. To me planned parenthood represents a mentality with regard to human development, which is of equal importance to rich and poor countries.

Our main "Dilemma for Affluents," it seems to me, is how to get rid of the idea of "giving aid," because it preserves the dangerous illusion in affluent societies of being safe and superior. How are we going to create in affluent populations a mentality capable of grasping the fact, so obvious to some of us, that in giving this so-called aid we are helping ourselves as much as we are helping others?

DISCUSSION FOLLOWING FOURTH SESSION

In the course of introducing Dr. Keenleyside, the Chairman, the Honourable Donald Macdonald made the following statement:

"In this coming week it is my expectation that a bill will be introduced into the Parliament of Canada by the present government to bring about the removal of the legal inhibitions which, since 1892, have bedogged those interested in family planning in Canada. It is my hope that that bill will pass and . . . . soon. But, having achieved that change in our domestic scene, we are then presented with an international challenge." [1]

These remarks were greeted with applause and are referred to a number of times by speakers and discussants.

Mr. Macdonald:

Dr. Cowan recommended that we stabilize our population in Canada. One of the truisms of public affairs in Canada has an under—rather than an over-population problem. It seems to me that Dr. Cowan was challenging two basic propositions, first that we should have a higher rate of immigration into this country, and second, to borrow a phrase from a friend of mine, that the state has no place in the bedrooms of the nation. Would you comment both as regards immigration policy and government measures for population control.

Dr. Cowan:

My concern is with stability, and this would apply to immigration and to population control. I agree with the comment of your esteemed friend. His intent was quite different from what I have been talking about.

Questioner:

It has often been proclaimed that mental illness and suicide in Sweden is a consequence of Swedish policy with regard to abortion and contraception. Would Dr. Sjövall comment on the validity of this claim?

Dr. Sjövall:

There is not the slightest objective support of such a statement. I do not really know whether our suicide rate is very much higher than in other

European countries at the moment. The Swedes have fairly accurate statistics. We are pretty sure that suicides in Sweden are registered as such, whereas I am not sure that this is so in all countries.

Questioner:

This afternoon I understood Dr. Colin Clark to say that only with a growing population can a country prosper. I found this very disturbing. Would Dr. Keenleyside care to comment?

Dr. Keenleyside:

First of all, I am not a professional economist. I have had some practical experience in some of these things but that's about all. Can a country go on indefinitely increasing its GNP? When it comes to the point of stopping, what happens? Does the society collapse, or is there some other solution for it? I simply don't agree with the statement as it was presented.

Questioner:

Dr. Cowan stated that the integrity of our environment must be maintained and he made references to pollution. I thought of the 300,000 chemicals in our air mentioned by Dr. Cole in an earlier session. It is basically our technology that is doing this. Now people are asking for further technology and science to treat this problem. This technology would in turn have its own produce and it is possible that an endless cycle is being created. Processes to combat pollution will have their own pollutants, and we may have entered into an impossible task. Would Dr. Cowan comment as an ecologist on our chances of creating some sort of balanced ecological cycle.

Dr. Cowan:

The destruction of the environment is not solely a population problem. It is a question of a technological increase, of the social attitudes towards how we use our technology in our interests. I can envision that some of our apparent solutions will, as you suggest, produce other problems unique to them.

However, we don't need a great deal of research to do far better than we are doing now. It has been stated that the main block to getting on with the task of pollution abatement lies not in the research laboratories of the nation but in the board rooms of public and private concerns. The questions asked there are not really about environmental integrity but of the *immediate* advantage of the distributors or users of the goods and products. I don't think we should envision any return to a simplistic balance. We may have to do some serious rethinking about how we handle such things as domestic sewage. Is there any real reason why we have to flush away six ounces of urine with 50 times as much water? I really don't see the sense of it, particularly when water is a very scarce commodity in large parts of the world. There are other answers to problems than those we are applying today, this is what all of us must see.

Questioner:

Canada and other "just societies" have on occasion made food available to starving peoples. Food could be grown on good land but is not grown in order to avoid excess crops. Would Dr. Keenleyside please tell us how there can be excess food crops when two-thirds of the world's people do not have enought to eat?

Dr. Keenleyside:

First of all the situation changes from year to year. Three years ago in India they were over the verge of starvation in many areas in that country. These past two years there has been a marked increase in their crops and the demand for relief food from outside, particularly from North America, has been greatly reduced.

The situation in general is complicated by the fact that it's not only a matter of production of the crop but also of the means of distribution. The long-term situation is dependent upon whether the population in such a country will continue to escalate. If the demand for food is going to increase, as many observers believe that it will, it may well be that existing surpluses can meet the shortages in all needy countries in the world, at least if we work out some system of distribution. But in the long-term it is quite apparent to those who have studied the problem from the viewpoints of production, distribution, and population growth that the availability of food will not be adequate to take care of the growing population. If people in such areas act to reduce their rate of population growth the situation can eventually be stabilized.

Questioner:

It was with great interest that we noted that Canada, after such a belated number of years, had begun its approach toward a policy of planned families which Sweden has been doing since before the Second World War.

On the other matter, Canada has one of the largest wheat production lands and agricultural bases in the world and I would appreciate it if Mr. Macdonald could explain to us something about the proposed new International Development Institute which was mentioned with a flourish

177

in the papers some months ago as a centre for promoting research and development to assist the developing countries. More specifically, will the high-protein research work that has been done by the universities, especially in Guelph and Winnipeg, be incorporated in this programme?

Mr. Macdonald:

It is the responsibility of one of my colleagues to announce the programmes under that proposal as they are formulated. With respect to the development of higher yield strains of wheat and higher yield strains of other cereals, I think it is generally recognized both by the Canadian Government and other producing governments that over the long run the solution to the under-feeding problem is going to have to come from the developing countries themselves. However, over a shorter run, one of the aspects of the international grains agreement has been to provide a vehicle whereby the four principal producer and exporter countries, of which Canada is one, will be able to make large quantities of cereals available to developing countries, large quantities of cereals which will essentailly be funded by the contributions of other nations. I would make a comment about a reference made by the previous questioner with regard to the utilization of the Canadian agricultural lands and the transfer of surpluses of any edibles from Canada, and as far as that goes, from any other producer country to the developing countries. It is true that there may well be vacant lands, there may well be surpluses involved, but notwithstanding their availability there is still an economic cost involved for the producer-nation in doing that, and it was in order to spread the responsibility that the assistance of non-producer nations was invited. For example, arrangements were made under the international grains agreement to have Canadian, Argentinian, United States, and Australian wheat and other grains made available on the world market.

Questioner:

A brief observation to which Dr. Cowan and perhaps his fellow British Columbian might react. It seems to me that your global perspective was underlined by a kind of assumption that the world can be divided into two lots of people, one of which has come to grips with technology and therefore is affluent, and the other which has failed to do so and is therefore poor and over-populated. This strikes me as a historical and paternalistic and rather less of an organic view than I would expect an ecologist to come up with. I would put it to you that the relations between the rich and the poor sections of the world have been rather intimate for some time and continue to be so increasingly, and that we are all involved in one economic and technologic organism in which some

178

people impoverish others. What is to be done has more to do with changing that organism drastically than it has to do with mere further sharing, much less laying down the law à la Robert MacNamara.

Dr. Cowan:

I agree quite substantially with some parts of your statement. My intent was to point out the existing situation and the historical background to it, that the advanced technologies have been developed in a very small part of the world. The very advance of these technologies has made it possible for these parts of the world to take advantage of resources which they extracted from a very large part of the world, as we were reminded by earlier speakers. We can certainly regard this as inequitable. We had clearly pointed out to us the anachronism in which the economic strength of some of the already food-rich nations is being used to buy food from impoverished nations that already have food shortages. This is one of the extraordinary anachronisms of our inter-dependent world situation that I know you resent and I resent. We are trying to find the mechanisms to do something about his kind of thing. I would agree with you that the world of today and increasingly the world of tomorrow is an interconnected web. If those now impoverished cannot have any substantial part of it, inevitably this leads to the impoverishment of all of us. An essential part of any global concept must be to try and equate access to the world's resources, but as has been indicated by all the speakers so far this is a very complicated task and there are no simplistic solutions.

Dr. J.M. Robson:

My question is for you, Mr. Macdonald. You have already dealt with two of the matters on which the Teach-In has focussed—the population question and, more recently, the matter of sharing resources in so far as you felt it possible for you to speak. I was tempted to ask you to assure us that you would take a third focus to your good friend and to your other colleagues in the Cabinet and to Parliament as a whole, namely the question of how to prevent the affluent society from being merely an effluent society, but I am assured from your attitude as a whole that you will raise this matter as well. The question I think that each of the Teach-Ins has raised and this one in a very dramatic way is the question for each of us here. As citizens you know that apathy is one of the marks of the Canadian populace and one cause of that apathy is certainly the feeling that no matter how sincere our actions, we find it difficult to influence the government. Could you, Sir, very briefly suggest ways in which people who have become concerned might express that concern effectively?

179

Mr. Macdonald:

Every effort to reach myself and other elected representatives and to put the point of view forward will have the effect of keeping us well aware not only of the importance of the issue but of your emphasis on the importance of the issue. What may not be so obvious is the need for addressing yourselves, if I may say so, with a tolerant and sympathetic attitude but nonetheless with your own conviction to those of us in our community who don't happen to share your particular viewpoint on this question. In the long run just as a political consensus has developed in the direction of a change of our domestic law so political consensus must develop as well to Canada's role in this matter abroad. I recognize the responsibility of the legislature and particularly of the executive to take the leadership in this consensus, but you can make a great contribution by also persuading consent from those who do not at the moment agree with our point of view.

Questioner:

Dr. Keenleyside, if we are to put our own house in order, would you care to comment on our immigration policy. We drain off the best of the other countries; we do not accept their worst. This is hyprocritical. Must we say no to all or yes to all?

Dr. Keenleyside:

I shall attempt a quick answer to your question. It wouldn't be a great help to the persons concerned from other countries nor to our own society to remove the barriers completely for anyone who wanted to come in. It may be that at some stage if populations continue to grow around the world we will be forced to take that position. Certainly it is very likely that the pressure on our immigration barriers will increase in the years to come.

We have opened the barriers from time to time to take in quite a few people who would not normally have been acceptable at all. However, it is certainly true that we do run a discriminatory immigration policy. I think it is not only morally right but I think it is going to be politically imperative that we change that in the years to come. Whether Dr. Cowan would approve of that kind of a movement or not is open to question, but whether he thinks it is a good thing or a bad thing, I think it is inevitable.

Questioner:

Dr. Keenleyside referred to the situation in Canada, particularly to Section 150 of the Criminal Code relating to preventing conception, and advocated a change in ecclesiastical attitude, of an attitude in the churches. I am sure he is familiar with the hearings of the House of Commons Committee on Public Welfare a year or two ago. Would he tell us of the presentations made before that Committee advocating a change in the law by revision of Section 150 by the United Church of Canada, the Anglican Church of Canada, the Presbyterian and Baptist Churches of Canada, the Canadian Council of Churches, the Clergy Advisory Committee, the Planned Parenthood of Toronto, as well as also the Canadian Catholic Congress. I am sure he is familiar with the findings and hearings of the Committee, and will he inform us precisely the attitude taken by these various Church bodies?

Dr. Keenleyside:

I think the questioner has answered his own question really. It is true that these various bodies appeared and with varying degrees of enthusiasm and force presented recommendations to the government looking towards the action that has now been decided upon and in accordance with Mr. Macdonald's announcement is shortly to be acted upon. In what I said earlier on I intended to suggest that we should assist those persons in Canada who are trying to influence the remaining ecclesiastical objectors to the change in he law. There are some, not only some portions of the Roman Catholic Church, but also other religious organizations that are opposed to that change. My suggestion was that we should do what we properly can to influence the persons and organizations concerned to change their views.

Questioner:

Dr. Cowan, I assume one of the themes of your address to be that we must address ourselves as a nation to consider the quality of our Canadian environment and its intrinsic value as a source of recreation and to show more respect to natural balances and to processes on which we are far more dependent than we may realize. The problem that arises in my mind is that such considerations involve a conflict with so-called technological progress and more often than not lose out because they cannot readily be measured on a monetary scale and thus tend to be ignored in consideration of otherwise economically appealing developments such as hydro projects. My question is: How can natural values compete with a simplistic profit motive in an industrial society with primarily a dollar and cents conception of and approach to development?

Dr. Cowan:

The operations of a democratic society such as ours depend in essence upon the public vision of what is tolerable and what is desirable,

181

and though the people who are concerned with the protection of the environment get horribly discouraged by finding themselves continually backing up, I think that most of us would be prepared to admit that on the North American continent we are no longer backing up quite so fast. There have been some really monumental achievements that haven't been given nearly enough publicity in the last few years. I would like to point for instance to the cleaning-up of San Francisco Bay. Five years ago San Francisco Bay was a stinking cesspool and I make that comment in complete accuracy. The San Francisco Bay of today is unrecognizable to those of us who knew it five years ago, and this was done by an organized group of people including industrialists, ecologists, sociologists, and all the kinds of people that it takes to make a great city community. Similarly, the experiences of the Nature Conservancy of Britain fills one with admiration. It is possible to do these things and it is possible to engage industrialists in doing these things once they realize it is just jolly good business to do them. I think the mission of so many others is to counteract an attitude that was reflected by Norman Cousins in an article in the *Saturday Review*. He says, "A nation conditioned by affluence might possibly be suffering from compassion fatigue, or from conscience sickness, the peril of narrowing our field of vision to leave out the view of life disfugured by hunger and poverty whose living systems and finest landscapes are being destroyed by wanton, ignorant or misguided people." It is the mission of all of us that are concerned to make quite sure that our nation doesn't suffer from compassion fatigue and from a lack of vision and conscience.

Questioner:

Dr. Sjövalll, why don't people just give things such as excess food away, and I stress the words, just give it away?

Dr. Sjövall:

You ask me why they don't give it away. As a psychological problem you mean? Now that's a hard one. I don't feel capable of answering it. My knowledge of human nature has not given me the impression that there are any people with the kind of attitude that leads them to just give things away. I don't think this phenomenon exists in humanity.

Mr. Macdonald:

I call upon Dr. Falls who will say the final words at the Teach-In.

Dr. Falls:

Our thanks go to Mr. Macdonald. I think that even a year ago it would have been difficult to have senior member of the government here on such an occasion and I was, as the rest of you were, encouraged by his attitude and his words tonight. Our thanks also to all the speakers in all the sessions, to all the chairmen and to all those who have helped with this Teach-In.

I said in introducing the Teach-In that I was worried and the discussions we have heard have not lessened my concern. You will understand why I as an ecologist am concerned, but what I feel is not really very important. The question is for you who have listened to the talks and to the discussions. What do you think? Do you think there is a crisis of numbers? Do you think it is urgent? What do you think we as Canadians can do about it? Do you think the problems and solutions are political, ideological, economic or philosophical, or is it possible there are also underlying biological limitations with which the other issues have to come to terms?

I hope this will be the beginning of more serious consideration and discussion by Canadians of issues of population and related matters both at home and abroad.

1. — In May, 1969, the Canadian Parliament removed certain provisions of the Criminal Code which had the effect of making it no longer an offence to advertise or sell contraceptives.

In September, 1970, the federal Minister of Health announced that funds would be made available to public and private agencies to expand family planning services in Canada. At the same time, the Minister for External Affairs announced that Canada would provide assistance to international agencies concerned with population programmes abroad. At first, most of these funds would be channelled through the United Nations. *The editors.*

Summary of Discussion by Radio Panel

Mr. Ron McKee:

Dr. Regier mentioned some statistics to us a moment ago. We have watched a tally board here relating the change of population over this weekend.

Dr. Regier:

The rate of increase in the world's population is about two per second. It's a nice small number and it's nothing to get alarmed at of course. The ticker over there has been tallying up the numbers as we have been going, and I have been wondering how to get some sort of an idea of the size of this number. We started this Teach-In just a little over two days ago, just a little bit over 50 hours ago. At two per second this means that our population *increase* in the period of this Teach-In was just a little over one-third of one million. If we have hopes that about 20 percent of these people will be educated at university level, in technology or arts or science, just a nice moderate 20 percent, then of course we will have to build three new universities the size of the University of Toronto just to accommodate the *net increase* in number of children during the last two days. The University of Toronto is reputedly the largest university in the Common-wealth, so we'll have to build three universities the size of the largest university of the Commonwealth to accommodate the excess children born during this Teach-In. This is just one sort of institution that we'll have to build; this will be only a small part of the cost involved in accommodating this two-days' increase in the world population. Perhaps this gives us some idea of the size of the task facing us.

Mr. McKee:

Astonishing figures.

Mr. Cadbury, the Chairman of the third session, is with us. I ask him to comment on the IPPF of which he is an officer.

Mr. Cadbury:

The International Planned Parenthood Federation is a Federation of 54 full country members and another 30 countries with which we deal. This is an international voluntary organization. The Family Planning Federation of Canada is the Canadian component of that International, with a number of associations across the country. It's still a very young and very small organization and frankly it is a little bit of an embarrassment to some of us who have been working in the international field for some years that so far our own country has only been able to

184

mount such a small effort. But that, you see, is because of our law. Canadian law now prohibits the advertising, selling, or giving advice on methods to prevent conception. The announcement by Mr. Donald Macdonald that the government of Canada is going to introduce reform legislation is opening an entirely new era. If the reform goes far enough, then the days in which we have had to be embarrassed by a small Canadian operation may hopefully be over. The smallness of our operation is partly financial and I should perhaps just add a little footnote that the existence of the prohibition in the law also meant that no official action has been taken, no allowance on income tax for donations for this purpose has been allowed, and frankly we have been working on a shoestring.

Mr. McKee:

Can we assume then, from some of Dr. Sjövall's statements about money from his country going to support this Federation, that Swedish money has been coming to Canada?

Mr. Cadbury:

Yes that's true. Something like that we don't like to voice too loudly because we are really rather ashamed of it but that is a fact that the international organization has had to help the Canadian organization because, due to our peculiar legal situation, we couldn't help ourselves. That is an embarrassing situation for a country like Canada. When we can finally raise some money the first thing we can do is repay that loan with interest so that Canada will be helping other countries.

Mr. McKee:

Dr. Wingell was a member of the Programme Committee of the Teach-In and is a Professor at St. Michael's College. Can we invite your comments as a Catholic on aspects of this Teach-In?

Dr. Wingell:

I imagine that persons seeing two Catholics involved in this Teach-In taking opposite positions will be subject to a certain amount of confusion. One thing may be pointed out: the so-called Conservative, Colin Clark, actually chose to display strife within the Church, even to boast that he was a member of the minority that got the ear of Paul VI so to speak, whereas the so-called liberal Dr. Dupré, tried to take an all-inclusive view rather than heightening or even representing division within the Church. Dr. Dupré spoke, I think, from a Conservative position. He tried to state that on which all Catholics agree, namely that on a moral teaching not contained in divine revelation, which is issued by the ordinary teaching

185

authority of the Church, dissent is perfectly possible. On moral issues like these subjective assent is required or pre-supposed if there is going to be any objective morality. In other words he took the same position that the Canadian bishops have expressed. They similarly did not talk about the morality or immorality of artificial contraception; they treated only of our response to the Encyclical and said they left particularly theologians, scientists, intellectuals, Catholic men of education, quite free to dissent and disagree. If we look at the brief of the Canadian Catholic bishops to the House of Commons Standing Committee on Public Welfare we have to realize that leadership structures of the Church are definitely open to proposals such as we heard tonight, and the problem then is really one of education and communication within the Church itself.

Dr. Regier:

I would like to go back, Dr. Wingell, to our deliberations last spring in the Teach-In Programme Committee deciding on what to do with the so-called Catholic issue. We talked it over as a group, Catholics and non-Catholics, and decided it really wasn't likely to be a live issue by the time of the Teach-In in the fall. So we didn't actually have the "Catholic issue" on the program. We had planned to ask Dr. Dupré to speak about Christian ethics. We were surprised during the summer when the Encyclical appeared in a form quite different from what we had expected. And so we scrambled to bring the "Catholic issue" back in. Now, looking back on what's happened here these last few days, do you think it was a good decision?

Dr. Wingell:

I suppose in a way it was necessary in view of the publicity that the Encyclical got, but I personally resent being constantly distracted to the discussions of issues like these. Sexual morality is after all on the fringe of Christian values so far as I can see. There are more important questions to Christians, or there are questions which *should be* much more important to Christians, such as social justice, charity, the brotherhood of man, and even more so the meaning of the life of Christ, the incarnation, and so on. But I think, all in all, that the shape of Catholic opinion has become clearer at this Teach-In. I think it was necessary for us to include both sides because after all the weight of traditional structure of authority did rest with Paul VI when he issued that Encyclical. I want to see what the papacy and the Roman bureaucracy decide to do about the statement of nearly all the national episcopates and all the national bishops. I regret that these problems internal of the evolution of the Catholic Church should have such an unfortunate effect on the public scene.

186

Mr. Cadbury:

As a non-Catholic and very actively involved in Planned Parenthood affairs, I think it was a good thing to have this discussion. It probably cleared the air a good deal, but our experience, I hope it's not offensive to say this, is increasingly that it doesn't really much matter what the Roman Catholic Church thinks about this question. I participated in the largest Conference there has ever been on population, in Santiago, Chile, just a year ago, there we had 1200 delegates, enormous interest, and enthusiasm from all the Latin-American countries, and of course the audience was almost entirely Catholic in its religious allegiance. The question of the Catholic attitude to family planning was not mentioned. There were priests in the audience, there were priests who spoke, but the question of what the Catholic Church thought about the question just wasn't considered a matter that was going to have to be discussed. Now I hope that that will relieve some of our Catholic friends from a problem; it certainly relieves us, and I think perhaps that is the way we all hope it will end.

Dr. Wingell:

I suggest that the experience Mr. Cadbury had was really a discovery of what the Catholic Church did think about the problem. It became clear that the laity, the priesthood, the people who possessed experience in working with these problems, had a certain view. Really it was what Rome thought that didn't matter.

Mr. Cadbury:

Our problem now is with the politicians rather than with the clergy. I am so delighted that today we have had a politician coming out so positively. The problem has been more with Protestant politicians than with Catholic ones, because the former seem to be more afraid of the odd vote that they will lose than the man who is severely entrenched in his relations with his electorate and their religious affiliations. It is rather noteworthy that in Canada today society is moving further and faster in Quebec than in other places. In the city of Montreal the city opened nine clinics which give family planning advice, in the city of Toronto there are none. Toronto will not do it. In the province of Quebec the government gives a fee to a doctor giving family planning advice in their provincial health insurance scheme. No other province does this.

Mr. McKee:

Dr. Stycos said that Canada did not have a bad imperalist international reputation. Now what shade of grey are we?

187

Mr. Cadb

at dif   passports
passp   anadian
more   ome in
over   true all
in th   es went
Com   all the
which   nation
activ   all our
that.   onfirms
those   e from

othe   olicy in
Cana   people
to c   ave the
swif   re that
they   ey are
bless

Mr.   g and I

since